Original Student Monologues

Auditions, Competitions, Festivals, and Class.

GARY ALAN BAKER JR.

Awkwardly Silent Productions LLC.

D1282674

ISBN-13:9798627447827

Library of Congress Control Number: 2020095494
Printed in the United States of America

DEDICATION

Dedicated to my wonderful students and their equally amazing parents.

CONTENTS

Title Page
Copyright
Dedication
Contents
Categories
Foreward
Preface

1   Adventures in getting   1
my ears pierced

2   Awkward Break- in   3

3   Becky the Babysitter   5

4   Betrayal   7

5   Bookmark Birthdays   9

6   Brian   11

7   Bridges   13

8   Brother's Territory   15

9   Bunny Expectations   17

10   Callbacks   19

11   Charm   21

12   Cheetos   22

13   Class President   24

14   Clear Communication   26

15   Cute and Cuddly   28

16   Dislocated   29

17   Double Dip   31

18   Down Home Southern   33
Cooking

19 Emma   35

20 Flirty   37

21 Fundraiser   39

22 Gamers Anonymous   41

23 Girl Scout Cookies   43

24 History 101   45

25 Imaginary Friend Party   47

26 Investigator   49

27 Limited Time Offer   51

28 Loaf of Bread   53

29 Lola   55

30 Love and Fear   56

31 Madam Cynthia   57

32 Melody   59

33 Mom's Presentation   61

34 Never Stop Believing   63

35 Online French Class   65

36 Pageant   67

37 Play Practice   69

38 Preparing for a Pet   71

39 Pushed   74

40 Right thing to do   76

41 Slime   77

42 Sports   78

43 Sprinkles   79

44 Story Time   81

45 Sunshine Girl   83

46 Theatre Etiquette   85

47 The Most Amazing   87
    Harold!

48 The Funeral   90

49 Travel Stories   91

50 Tryouts   93

51 Twins   95

52 Visiting Hours   97

53 Warm-ups   99

CATEGORIES

FEMALE COMEDY:
Adventures in Getting My Ear's Pierced
Awkward Break-in
Becky the Babysitter
Betrayal
Bookmark Birthdays
Brother's Territory
Bunny Expectations
Cheetos
Class President
Clear Communication
Cute and Cuddly
Dislocated
Down Home Southern Cooking
Flirty
Girl Scout Cookies
Limited Time Offer
Madam Cynthia
Mom's Presentation
Pageant
Play Practice
Sprinkles
Story Time
Theatre Etiquette
Travel Stories

FEMALE DRAMATIC:
Brian
Bridges
Charm
Emma
Lola
Love and Fear
Melody
Pushed
Right thing to do
Sunshine Girl
Visiting Hours

MALE COMEDIC:
Double Dip
Gamers Anonymous
History 101
Online French Class
Preparing for a Pet
Slime
The Most Amazing Harold!
Tryouts
Warm-ups

MALE DRAMATIC:
Callbacks
Never Stop Believing
Sports

MALE/FEMALE: COMEDIC
Fundraiser
Imaginary Friend Party
Investigator
The Funeral

MALE/FEMALE: DRAMATIC
Loaf of Bread
Twins

FOREWORD

Now that you have purchased this book, you are able to use any monologue contained within for auditions, acting competitions, acting festivals, or in class. You are allowed to change the wording and/or cut any monologue for time constraints. Just make sure the overall idea of the monologue is still intact

Each monologue was originally written with competitions and auditions in mind. All monologues have been effective in bringing home high scores and/or bookings.

DO NOT RECORD MONOLOGUES AND POST ON THE INTERNET!

Contact us at the email below for information on how to get an original monologue written just for you.

GBMonologues@gmail.com

PREFACE

As part of being an acting instructor, it's my job to find material that really fits my students. Over the years, I've noticed that it has become increasingly difficult to find monologues and scenes that are appropriate, have a good storyline, or fit my student's personalities. So, I decided to start writing original material from ideas discussed during student's lessons. Since then, we have seen an increase in scores and film projects booked from these monologues. If I was having trouble finding monologues for my students, what was it like like for student's who are on their own looking for material? This is why I think it was important to publish the material that has been so successful for my students.

ADVENTURES IN GETTING MY EARS PIERCED

Picture it! Jacksonville, Florida. 2021. Me, a girl just wanting to get her ears pierced for her 9th birthday. My mother, blocking me from doing so because of a tradition in my family, dating back to before I was born. The tradition that states women in our family have to wait until they are ten years old to get their ears pierced. You can imagine the emotional state I was in. Being locked in the house for what seemed like the entire year of 2020, let's not talk about that though. And now, businesses were opening, life was getting somewhat back to normal. And the Claire's down the street started doing piercings again! I begged my mother once more, "PLEASE, let me get my ears pierced!," and to my surprise, she agreed…as long as I stopped eating her secret stash of chocolate that she hides from Dad. I guess I wasn't being as stealthy as I thought?

Anyway, I agreed and we had a deal. The next morning, we picked up my best friend Caroline and her mother, because I'm not going to go get my ears pierced without my best friend by my side! Nothing could stop us now! Or so I thought. As we pulled onto the expressway our car slowed to a stop. "What's happening?!" I yelled as my mother put the car in park. "Looks like someone is broken down a few cars in front of us and their car is blocking the lanes, sweetheart." my mother said. My brain was silently exploding inside my head. I looked frantically all around, certainly someone could help this person move their car! "WE HAVE PLACES TO BE PEOPLE!" I just knew in my heart that we would miss our appointment and Claire's would be booked for the next year because of all the other little girls who had

1

to go without getting their ears pierced during the pandemic. Then, when all seemed lost, something magical happened. A large man suddenly appeared and charged right past us towards the broken down car. He reminded me of Jack Black, but if Jack Black played a superhero with a long gray beard. I pressed my face against the glass of the window to get a better view. I saw Jack Black run up to the broken down car. He did a sort of pose like one of those Greek God statues (She does this pose). Then he put his large hands on the back of the car. He was using all of his strength to push it to the side of the road. It was just him pushing the car and this little old lady steering. Finally, the car was clear. The little old lady gave him a hug and then he turned and started running back. His long gray beard hair blowing behind him in the wind. You could see the little old lady, with a relieved tear in her eye, reach out one arm towards him and have one on her heart as she watched him trot from her. As he ran past our car, everything seemed to be in slow motion. I noticed a glimmer from his ear lobes. Both of his ears were pierced! I couldn't believe it! He winked at us as he passed our car and then I watched as superhero Jack Black ran up to the car behind us and dive headfirst through the open window. This would have been super impressive except for the fact that he got stuck in the window and his legs were just kind of kicking in the air as he was trying to pull himself through. The traffic started to clear and my mom put our car in drive. Caroline and I looked at each other in shock and awe at what we just saw. There was no doubt in our minds that we were making the right decision to get our ears pierced. With our ears pierced we could do anything, just like Superhero Jack Black. Our moms have since made us promise to stop trying to jump in the window of our cars when they pick us up here at school though. This was a good idea because sometimes it's hard to tell if the car windows are open and it really hurts when they're not. Anyway, I see my mom pulling up, but I can't wait until Monday to see what decision you make about getting your ears pierced this weekend! Just think to yourself, "What would Superhero Jack Black do?" Okay, bye!

Originally performed by: Kennedy F. 2022

AWKWARD BREAK - IN

(Girl stumbles on stage dressed in pajamas and rain boots. She has accidentally fallen through the window of her neighbor's upstairs bedroom and is trying to find her way out of their house. Suddenly, she turns to see her neighbors, Mr. and Mrs. Reid, staring at her.)

Oh! Hi Mr. and Mrs. Reid! I know it might seem shocking to see me here…in your house…at 10PM…with branches in my hair, but I promise there is a really good, rational explanation. You see, I was in my house watching a rerun of *Murder She Wrote*, because I love mysteries, and right when they were about to get to the juicy "who-dun-it" part, I started hearing a weird noise outside my window. I paused my Netflix and peering through the blinds in my living room, I saw my cat Mr. Snickers stuck in your tree. So, being the problem solver that I am, I put on my boots and headed outside. I tried to keep the cat calm as I approached the tree. I carefully, ever so slowly climbed from one branch to the next until I was finally in arms reach of Mr. Snickers. I stretch out my arms to grab the cat and that's when I came to the horrible realization that this wasn't Mr. Snickers at all… it was Brad Lunsford's cat Hurricane! If you've ever met Hurricane, you know that he isn't exactly the cuddling type. I'm sure he saw the fear in my eyes as clearly as I was seeing the anger in his. After what seemed like hours, I decided to make my move to get down out of the tree. I slowly lowered one leg down to a branch below. This was a sturdy branch that held my weight quite nicely. The cat stayed extremely still. I then lowered my other leg onto another branch below. This branch was not as strong and as it snapped, Hurricane lost his mind! He lunged forward hitting me in the stomach. Which, in turn, caused me to fall backwards through your upstairs window busting out the screen. And not to change the topic, but can I just say that you have a beautiful bedroom, the colors are so complimentary.

(Seeing that they are becoming more upset)

I promise that this is the last time you will see me in your house unexpectedly. I know I said this the last two times it happened, but THIS time I mean it! Now, if you'll excuse me, I'll go and get the check from my. Mom to pay for your window screen I busted out. Goodnight Mr. and Mrs. Reid!

Originally performed by: Parker P. 2017. High Gold Award
Performed by: Brynne. 2018. High Gold Award
Performed by: Audrey H. 2019. High Gold Award

BECKY THE BABYSITTER

First of all I would like to thank you for the opportunity to become your babysitter. Gillian did a great job explaining why she would be a good pick as your son's baby sitter and now I hope you will give me just as much of your attention as you gave her. I have prepared a small scene that represents what a typical first meeting between your child and I would look like.

(She prepares herself by taking in a deep breath)

Now, you listen to me you little turd! Your parents left me in charge. Do you know what that means? DO YOU KNOW WHAT THAT MEANS!? It means that there is going to be no tom-foolery in this house. It means you will be in bed by nine P.M. It means that if you so much as look at me the wrong way, dinner won't be the delicious mac and cheese your parents left for you. No, it will be a basket of uncooked broccoli...WITH NO RANCH! I'm not like any other babysitter you've had before. I have the guts to follow through with my promises. Your parents can't help you now. You break anything in this house and your head will be buried in the sandbox outside. You talk back to me, I put you in a headlock and make you sing *Baby Shark "Do do do do do do."* You stay awake more than fifteen minutes after your bedtime, I make sure that the monsters come out from under your bed and watch you all night long.
1 I know what you're thinking, "Mom said there are no monsters under the bed." That's only because she doesn't know where to look.*1*
So, get ready for a night you won't forget, because Becky the

Babysitter is in charge!!!!

(Changes back into a pleasant young lady)

Thank you!

So, Mr. And Mr.s Grady, I hope I have given you enough to think about in reference to choosing who would be best to take care of your son. I'll expect a phone call in a couple of hours and I'm free Friday night. I'll just let myself out. Have a good night!

1 *(If Becky is younger and might be interviewing to babysit someone older than her)* I know what you're thinking, "I'm 15! You can't tell me what to do!" And to that I say, do you really want to test me?"

Originally Performed by: Qwyn C. 2017. High Gold Award
Performed by: Alayna M. 2018. High Gold Award

BETRAYAL

Rebecca! I can't believe what Khloe just said to me! My mind can't process the horrible words that just came out of her mouth. Especially since we are supposedly her best friends. She knows how much it means to us! It's hard for me to even say it out loud, but I think you should hear it.

(She is so upset she pauses sporadically through the next sentence.)

Khloe said…that our favorite movie…IS GARBAGE! Can you believe that!? She called *"The Kissing Booth"* garbage, Rebecca! When she said that, all I could here were nails on a chalkboard just scratching down through our already fractured friendship. I say fractured because I still haven't forgiven her for bringing peanut butter cookies to school to share with everyone when she knows perfectly well that my third cousin removed, Charlie, is allergic to peanuts and I stand in solidarity with him. I don't care if he has never gone to this school or that he turned thirty-five last year. Actions speak louder than words Rebecca! Both Khloe's actions and words have offended me beyond measure. To say that the beautiful love story that the Kissing Booth portrays is trash? What kind of monster would say that? I would gladly fail all my classes just to watch Joey King and Jacob Elder slowly embrace…

(She's imagining it)

… and then the camera spins three hundred and sixty degrees as they finally kiss…AT THE KISSING BOOTH! It's the most perfect,

7

beautiful, amazing story ever told in the cinematic arts!

Titanic? Pshhh…let it sink. The Notebook? "I wrote you three hundred and sixty-five letters. I wrote you every day for a year…it wasn't over, it still isn't over!" They killed a whole tree writing all those letters is what they did! "A Walk to Remember" with Mandy Moore?

(BEAT as she thinks about that example and how sad that movie was)

Actually, that movie was really sad. I'm sorry I brought that movie up…

The point I'm trying to make is that Khloe has gone too far this time. I'm not going to tell you who to be friends with, but I think you should seriously reconsider inviting Khloe to your sleepover this weekend. Do you really want that kind of negativity in your life?

(Checks the time)

I've got to go. My cousin Charlie, the one who is allergic to peanuts, is picking me up today. Wait until I tell him what Khloe said! He is not going to believe it!

Originally performed by: Bianca P. 2020. Platinum Award

BOOKMARK BIRTHDAYS

Birthdays are my favorite! They're like a bookmark to your life, a new chapter every three hundred and sixty-five days. Birthdays are filled with traditions, like going out to a favorite restaurant, or blowing out an extra candle to show that you've made through another year. Or, in my case, your uncle sends you a birthday card at the end of November, when your birthday was in early October. I love birthday traditions, but what I love more than anything are when the plans for your birthday go hysterically wrong. Like, that time I decided that I wanted to go volunteer at the zoo's annual "Spooktacular" event instead of having a traditional party. I got to dress up as a zombie ghost. It wasn't the scariest of costumes, but it was just spooky enough. Throughout the evening I walked the paths at the zoo interacting with guests and handing out candy. I was having so much fun!

Then, as the night was coming to a close, I saw a child and his mother that I hadn't interacted with yet. So, I walked up and said "Hello, little boy! Would you like a piece of candy?" The little boy turned his head towards me, his joyful face turn into one of terror and before his mother or I could do anything, the boy kicked me in the shin and took off towards the zoo's exit waving his arms in the air while yelling, "MONSTER!!!" His mother, running after him could be heard saying in a defeated voice said "Oh, not again..."

(Laughs, then serious)
Don't worry, they caught the kid before he got out of the zoo.

Another fun birthday experience was on my fifteenth birthday. I had a sleepover with all of my friends from school. We played all the normal sleepover games. You know, telephone, pillow fighting, talking about the guys we were crushing on at school. Well, as we were all tucking ourselves in to go to sleep, my friend Sarah saw my cat, Midnight, in the kitchen. She called for him to come to us in the living room where we all were gathered. Everyone loves Midnight. He's the sweetest cat. So, of course, we all started calling to him. Finally he emerged and pranced to the center of where we were all lying down. "Awe, he's so cute!", Lizzie Shorestein said. "Look at the baby!" said Kara Platt. We were all gushing over him and his cuteness. That is until Dana Smith noticed something. "What is that in his mouth?" She said in a "something doesn't seem right" kind of way. As if answering Dana's question, Midnight opened his mouth and dropped a mouse in front of us on the floor. We all sat there frozen in shock. Then, the mouse jumped to life! It started running around the room! I have never seen a group of girls scatter as quickly as I did that night.

So, yes, birthdays are about tradition and celebrating being alive one more year, but the thing I really enjoy about birthdays are the hysterical surprises that no one expects to happen. That and of course the month-late birthday cards from Uncle Paul.

Originally performed by: Olivia L. 2021.

BRIAN

(Enters holding flowers)

Hey, Brian.

(BEAT)

I don't really know what to say, except that I am so sorry for what happened. If I could go back in time and change what I said to you that day, I would. I'm pretty sure you said some things you didn't mean as well. You weren't your normal self that day and I shouldn't have gotten so upset over such a dumb, insignificant thing.

(BEAT)

I didn't realize you were hurting so badly. You always seemed so happy.

(BEAT)

I wish you would have talked to me, or anyone who would have listened. I wish you would have let someone know what was going on in your head. To be honest, sometimes I don't know what's going on in my brain either, but talking about it with people that I trust really has helped me get through those hard times.

(BEAT)

I miss you.

(BEAT)

The guilt of what I said to you when I was angry will be something I have to live with for the rest of my life. You were never a bad person or a pain to be around. You were a good friend and I wish I could have been a better friend for you. I hope wherever you are, you know that in my heart I loved the person you were, flaws and all.

(BEAT)

Rest well my friend.

BRIDGES

I get nervous going over bridges. I remember a time when I was three or four years old, my father took me on a walk in a park near our old house. This park had a lot of grassy fields, a playground with the largest slide you've ever seen, and people walking their dogs every day.

The park also had a small stream that flowed through it. In order to get from one side of the stream to the other you would have to cross a wooden bridge in the center of the park. Every time my father and I went to this park, we would go up this bridge, stop at the very top, and look over the edge. This day was the same as any other. We walked up the bridge, stopped at the top, and looked out over the stream and the rest of the park. I had my doll with me that day. Her name was Kiara. She was my favorite doll. For some reason, on this day, I got the idea to hold Kiara out over the side of the bridge. I held her out, looking at her unsuspecting face. Then, I got another idea, and before I knew it, I opened my fingers and let Kiara go. I watched her fall and splash into the quick moving water of the stream and then I laughed.

A couple of seconds later I realized what I had done. I turned to my father and I started yelling that Kiara had fallen into the water. Knowing that this was my favorite doll, my father scooped me up and we went down to the the stream to search for Kiara, but she had been swept away. She was gone.

(BEAT)

This memory will pop up at the most random times. I repeat every move of that day in slow motion. I think that's why I get nervous going over bridges. I try to stop panic attacks by doing breathing exercises or counting backwards from one hundred. A lot of times that helps, but sometimes I can't fight off the panic attack. I imagine myself in Kiara's shoes, being held out over the water. Then, the person who I trusted the most lets go of me. I fall in slow motion towards the cold, dark, blue water where I am engulfed and swept away...never to be found...being gone...forever.

(BEAT)

My parents thought that I would grow out of it, but that hasn't happened. So, they reached out to you in hopes that we can work through what happened that day.

(BEAT)

I just want to be normal.

Originally performed by Lara G. 2021.

BROTHER'S TERRITORY

(Enters stage with a bat and ball. She tosses the ball up in the air a couple of times, swings, and misses each time.)

Normally, I wouldn't be able to play out here in the backyard because it's considered my brother's "territory."

(Smacks her arm as if a there is a mosquito biting her)

He's always out here practicing one sport or another and when I want to come out here and play, Brian, that's my brother's name, is like "Get outta here! I gotta practice!" And I always yell, "OUTTA AND GOTTA AREN'T REAL WORDSA!" *(BEAT)* Anyway, he fell backwards while playing football and broke his butt.

When we were at the hospital, the nurse gave him some laughing gas and he was saying the weirdest things like: "Why's that purple elephant staring at me?" And "Are you going to eat the rest of that pork chop?" He even asked the nurse if she would slap him so that he could make sure that what he was experiencing was "real life." She said that she couldn't do that, but I know an opportunity when I see one and I wasn't going to throw it away. I got grounded for two weeks, but it was well worth it.

The doctors said he'd have to take it easy for a couple of months to make sure his butt heals correctly. So, I have at least two months of uninterrupted outside play and I'm taking full advantage of it!

So far I've been able to play baseball, football, croquet, *(slaps mosquito)* soccer, tennis, and paddle ball *(slaps mosquito)*. I had a princess party and a tea party with all the garden gnomes. I barely even notice the mosquitos anymore.

(See a mosquito flying and lands on her forehead. She slaps herself in the forehead)

Oww!

(Recovers)

And even though it is one hundred and two degrees outside with ninety-five percent humidity, I'm not going to miss this opportunity. Plus, I've got to work on my throwing arm so that when Brian's butt isn't broken anymore, maybe he'll want to play catch with me!

(Picks up ball, winds her arms up and throws, there is a glass shattering noise. She is in shock and is trying to figure out what to do)

BRIAN DID IT!...wait...uh oh, I'm going to be in so much trouble!

(Rushes off stage)

Originally performed by: Skyler W. 2020. High Gold Award

BUNNY EXPECTATION

Hello PetSmart employee. I am here today because your company sold me a bunny that did not meet my expectations of what a bunny is supposed to be and I'd like to file a complaint.

(Employee tries to respond, but child puts their finger up defiantly to stop them before they start)

First off, we drove four hours to get a specific bunny. This bunny was all white and furry and was promised to be at your store's other location...four hours away. The bunny we ended up getting was brown with white spots. I overlooked this issue because, as you millennials would say, it wasn't a "dealbreaker." When we purchased said bunny, a fellow employee said that the bunny wouldn't get any bigger than the cute cuddly fur ball that we were taking home that evening. That was also a lie. She's as big as a Maine Coon cat now!

(Employee tries to talk and again, child puts finger up to interrupt employee before they could start talking)

I wanted a bunny that would love me. I wanted a bunny that would cuddle with me on cold nights. I wanted a bunny that would eat a carrot out of my hand.

Samantha Harmond has a bunny. Her bunny does all of those things. All my bunny does is sleep!

I put a brand new drinking bowl in her enclosure and all she did was chew on it. When I tried to explain to her that it's for drinking out of, not chewing on, I swear that she looked me directly in the eyes, hopped to the side of the dish, and kicked it over with her hind legs…SHE NEVER LOST EYE CONTACT THROUGH THE ENTIRE ENCOUNTER! I don't think she even blinked.

(Put's up finger to interrupt employee for a third time)

I understand that this specific PetSmart did not sell me my bunny. I told you we had to drive over four hours to get her at another PetSmart location. HOWEVER, I don't think there is any way I can talk my mom into driving me another four hours to fix this. Now I need you to listen to me very carefully so we can work this out. Tomorrow afternoon at four PM sharp, my mother and I will be walking through that door. I am going to point at that bunny right there. The snowy, white bunny that just magically appeared in your store overnight. Then you are going to convince my mother that it would be the greatest idea in the world for my brown bunny with white spots to have a companion. You'll do this or I will set every animal in this PetSmart free.

Got it?

Good.

I'll see you tomorrow.

Originally performed by: Tatum M. 2020. Auditions

CALLBACKS

(Walks on stage with a piece of paper as if someone has just handed them a side to read)

Thank you for the opportunity to be in front of you one more time before you make the decision about the part. I've never done a cold reading before, but there's a first time for everything.

My name is Colton Jones and I am reading for the part of "Nathan."

(Takes a breath)

"You don't get to control who I become. I'm in control of my own life. You weren't here when I needed you. When you were here all you did was berate me, cut down my confidence, and use your words to beat the will to dream out of me. You've been a horrible mot...." *(Can't say the word "mother". Clears throat and tries again)* "You've been a horrible..." *(BEAT)* Sorry, I just...umm...I had a similar...a similar fight with my mom recently. We never really resolved anything. Though that encounter did actually lead me to come to this audition, so I guess something good came out of it. If I could just have a second to... *(Pulls himself together)*

"You don't get to control who I become. I am in control of my own life. You weren't here when I needed you. When you were here all you did was berate me, cut down my confidence, and use your words to beat the will to dream out of me. You've been a horrible mother! There, I said it. You've been a horrible mother and you don't deserve

19

to come back into my life after all this time. I'm leaving and if I never see your face again, I would be okay with that. I wish you nothing but the best and I truly hope you can turn your life around. Goodbye, Mother."

(Realizing all the emotions that he just went through.)

My name is Colton Jones. Thank you for this opportunity.

Originally performed by: Luke G. 2018. Platinum Award

CHARM

I thought we were friends! Friends don't make friends cheat on tests, they don't lie to each other, and they don't take something that means so much to the other and break it! That charm bracelet was the last thing my mother gave to me before she died and now it's gone. Each charm held a special memory with my mom. The time we went to the zoo and got to pet the giraffes. When we adopted our dog, Scottie, and the first time I travelled on an airplane. A memory went with every charm. When you snapped that bracelet from my wrist, I saw all those memories flying away. I wasn't fast enough to grab most of them before they went into the storm gutter. They're gone forever. I'll never get those charms back.

Of course this one didn't get lost with all the others. This was the one my mom got me when I told her I had a best friend at school. My first best friend…you. My mom was so happy that I finally had someone to call a friend. I'm going to keep this charm to remember my mom's love and happiness, but I'm also keeping it to remind me that someone I thought was a friend decided since I wouldn't help them cheat on a test they could destroy something so important to me.

One day I'll forgive you, but I will never forget how much pain you put me through.

Originally performed by: Kate 2018. High Gold Award

CHEETOS

Janelle, I know it's been about a week since we last talked, but I really need to address something with you. You're my friend and I thought it would be best to bring this up face to face instead of letting it fester making me more and more upset as time goes by. Last Friday, you did something that I really didn't appreciate. It is probably one of the worst things that anyone has ever done in my presence.

(BEAT)

You look confused. You might not remember this because it might not have seemed like that big of a deal to you, but it was to me. It really made me question if you actually appreciate me as a friend at all or if you are just taking advantage of my friendship.

(BEAT)

You still look confused, so I'm just going to come out and say it. Janelle, last Friday at lunch, you licked your fingers the entire time you were eating your Cheetos. You did this right in front of me. I thought the look on my face might make you take note and ask what was wrong, but right after you popped one of those crunchy air puff tubes in your mouth-hole, all you said was, "Vanessa, you don't look too good, do you need to go to the bathroom?" Then, as you looked me straight in the eyes, you licked each finger expecting a response from me. That moment seemed like hours. Watching you eat the orange-yellow dust from each cheesy finger slowly killed me on the inside.

BEAT)

You remember Mrs. Nancy? The incredibly nice, pretty, young librarian that used to work in the library at school? She had a secret. I found out this secret one day when I was checking out some books about Ernest Hemminway. The books were for the report we had to do in English class. She was telling me about how much she enjoyed his work. She then noticed one of the books I was about to check out and said she hadn't read that book before. So, of course, I let her look at the book more closely. She opened the book and before I could get a word out in protest, SHE LICKED HER FINGERS AND STARTED FLIPPING THROUGH THE PAGES! I reported her immediately to the front office and I don't think it's a coincidence that the next week she "Married a rich gentleman from England" and moved away, giving up on her library job.

(BEAT)

I don't want the same thing to happen to our friendship. So, I'm going to ask that from now on you refrain from *(trying not to throw up in her mouth)* licking your fingers. If you value our friendship, you will take this to heart.

(BEAT)

(Smiling) I'm so glad we had this talk! I feel like the weight of the entire world has been lifted off of me and now our friendship can continue to flourish. Just remember what I told you about Mrs. Nancy okay? See you in Algebra!

Originally performed by: Vanessa D. 2021.

CLASS PRESIDENT

Thank you for that introduction Principal Pratt, and good afternoon class of 20*(XX)*! I want to thank you all for this opportunity to speak with you today about hopefully becoming your Class President. I come wanting to take the helm and guide our class through the hurdles of the next two years here at Lincoln Elementary. The other two candidates have stated their cases, but I think you will agree that I would be the best candidate for the job based on three important factors: tradition, speaking up, and safety.

First let me speak on tradition. Just like the President that our elementary school is named after, *(holding hand to the side of her mouth as if telling a secret)* Abraham Lincoln, I believe in education, dedication, and hard work. When Lincoln was a young child he used to spend his allowance on books so that he could educate himself. As my friend Harper Young can attest, I too have spent my allowance on books. Many of these books have words like "inconceivable" and "unparalleled" in them, which are words we aren't supposed to learn for another three years!

Secondly, when I look around at the other candidates up on this stage, I see quiet people who aren't strong enough or willing enough to stand up for injustices in our school. As any teacher who has had me in their class can tell you, I am one of the loudest students they've ever encountered. Overhead fluorescent lighting hurting your eyes? Time to push for LED natural lighting. Cafeteria food bland and tasteless? Time to put together a tasty food task force. Not enough recess time? Let's push that time from thirty minutes to forty-five minutes. I promise you that I will not shut this mouth until these problems have been fixed!

Lastly, I would like to speak about safety and, of course, protecting our class from vampires.

(BEAT)

As I learned last week, out of all the monsters that might break into our school, vampires would definitely be at the top of the list. I am now fully versed on the different types of vampires and what their weaknesses are thanks to Mrs. Collins, who instructed the lesson on monsters last week. I really don't see any of the other candidates taking on the vampires when they arrive at our place of learning. I will make sure that a sharpened stake and a garlic bulb are in every classroom to protect each and every student here at Lincoln Elementary.

So, in conclusion, if you value tradition, speaking your mind, and safety against impending vampire doom, please vote for me!

Thank you!

Originally performed by: Lara G. 2021.

CLEAR COMMUNICATION

I have ADHD and I wanted to come out here and clear up a few things.

Having ADHD doesn't make me embarrassed, it's just a part of who I am. Some people might think that having this diagnosis means that there is something wrong with me, but it doesn't mean that at all. Sure, I'm really fidgety and change the topic of conversation a lot, but look at it this way. What if the topic we are discussing is boring? Then, when I change the subject, I'm actually saving us some time and saving us from boredom.

(BEAT)

You're welcome.

(BEAT)

I think it's actually the people without ADHD that need the help. I mean, people understand if someone has an allergy to something. In a restaurant they're not going to look at you twice for ordering a salad without nuts because you are allergic to them. But, if I'm in that same restaurant and my body feels like it has to move around a little more than the average person then there is a problem. That's called a double standard!

If you look at things from the point of view of a person with ADHD, then you might be able to understand how we can help you improve yourself! For instance, I want to be an actor when I grow up, so my Mom took me to get my headshots last week. The photographer started taking pictures and at one point he asked me to lower my chin. So I did. Obviously, if he wanted me to lower my whole head, including my chin, he would have said tilt your head down. But, he said lower your chin. So, in my brain, logically my chin is connected to my jaw which is a hinge joint that can be lowered. So I did this *(opens mouth)*. Which is exactly what the photographer asked me to do. But apparently it's not what he wanted. He should have been more clear.

Another time my Mom and I were shopping and she asked me if I wanted a shirt she found that we could take fifty percent off of. I laughed and asked, "Why would I want half of a shirt?" and "If I do get it, do I get to choose which fifty percent I get to to keep?" Apparently she meant fifty percent off the price…again, she, like the photographer, should have been more clear in their communication.

Communication is the key to understanding ADHD. We all live in the same world, but we see it from different angles. So, next time you see me fidgeting or hear me changing the topic of conversation, just know that my mind works a little differently than your and there is nothing wrong with that.

Originally performed by: Sky W. 2021.

CUTE AND CUDDLY

Okay, so that attempt at stopping them didn't work like I had planned. Now they're more angry and I think they may have breached the front door. They've become more aggressive since I stopped feeding them. It all started last week when I was going to the beach to meet my friend, Donna. When I was leaving the house, I locked the door and turned around to go to my car. Staring up from the ground right in front of me was a cute and furry little creature. I looked down at him and he looked up at me. His eyes seemed to say, "Please ma'am, I am so hungry! Could you give me something to nibble on?" I said to him, "Aw, I'm sorry little buddy. I don't have any nuts to give you and I'm off to the beach to meet my friend Donna, and she hates it when I'm late." The little fluff ball inched closer as if to say, "But, ma'am, I have baby fluff balls that need nourishment. Couldn't you go back inside your house and see if there are any scraps you could spare?" So, I said, "Maybe I'll pick you up a little something on the way home from the beach, okay?" Then, the cute and cuddly little guy came right up to my foot. "Wow!" I thought to myself, "this squirrel is very bold." Before I could do anything, the little demon jumped onto my foot and latched his teeth into my big toe. I screamed and shook my foot until he let go. As fast as I could, I ran to my car and drove to the minute clinic where the doctors clearly didn't understand the severity of the situation. Somehow squirrels have lost their fear of people. What's to stop them from grouping together to come after us all? We'll never see it coming! They know that we are weak when it comes to cute and cuddly animals. Don't let them do to you what they have done to me. We must work to stop the squirrels from taking over!

Originally performed by: Tess M. 2017. High Gold Award

DISLOCATED

Oh! Hey, Mom! Wow! You are looking great today! Did you do something different with your hair? No? Did you buy a new Trixie Mattel make-up pallet? Hmm... well something is definitely different and it's really awesome because you look great!

(Tries to put both thumbs up and then realizes that one of their arms is still by their side and quickly puts the working arm down)

So, remember when you told me not to climb the huge oak tree in the backyard because I'm clumsy and I would fall out of it and break my arm? Well, I climbed the huge oak tree, I am clumsy, I did fall out of the tree, and I don't want to say I broke my arm, but there is definitely something wrong with it...see?

(They look at the arm which is motionless)

I just tried to wave at you.

(Calmly) Oh, no mom. I don't think it's bad enough to warrant a trip to the hospital. We don't need to get them involved. I think all I need is a nice hot bath and maybe we can rub a lot of soap on it. That will make it all clean and help it to start working again.

(Getting nervous) No, really Mom, I'm okay. I mean we have two arms for a reason right? Just in case one arm stops working we have another one to pick up the workload. I can just use my other arm to do everything, watch!

(They pull out a piece of paper with horrible writing on it)

I've already started practicing writing with my other hand and I was surprised how good my penmanship is. See, this is my name!

(They are really scared because Mom isn't buying it and is getting ready to take them to the hospital)

No! Mom, please! I don't want to go to the hospital! Really, it's not that bad! *(BEAT)* What if they can't fix it and they want to cut it off?! *(BEAT)* Also, it will probably cost a lot of money that you could be using for spas or date nights with Dad...

(Panicing)

Please, Mom! Look! It doesn't even hurt!

(They push on their shoulder and their arm pops back into place. They look at their arms and yell. Then there is a slow realization that goes from yelling in pain to being happy that their arm has started working again.)

Would you look at that? I guess I just popped it out of place. Nothing to worry about. No reason to head to the hospital now. So, I'm just going to head back outside. I sure did learn a valuable lesson today. Okay, bye Mom!

Originally performed by: Kennedy F. 2020 High Gold Award

DOUBLE DIP

Rebecca! I'm so happy that you said yes to going on this date with me. It really means a lot. I didn't know Chili's was your favorite restaurant. That's pretty cool.

(Her father escorted her in)

Hello, Mr. Robins.

(Back to Rebecca)

I didn't expect for your father to come along too, but I guess that's alright. It means he loves you and wants to make sure you are safe.

(BEAT)

I ordered us some chips and queso while I was waiting for you to get here. I hope you like chips and queso. I guess I should have asked before I ordered it. I hope it's okay. It's really one of my favorite things on the menu. I could eat cheese all day. Am I talking a lot? When I get nervous I tend to just keep talking and talking and sometimes I even annoy myself. Let's talk about you! What kind of shows do you like to watch? Right now I'm really into *(insert any popular tv show)*. It's a really funny show about…

(Looks at Rebecca, then down at the queso dip, then back up at her)

I'm sorry, did you just? I mean, I saw you, but…I just need to make

31

sure that my eyes aren't playing tricks on me. Did you just double dip a chip that you put in your mouth?

(BEAT)

I…I just don't know what to say. Umm…I thought you were…you know…normal. But, what kind of person double dips a chip that they put in their mouth? Your spit touched that chip. Did you know that a humans mouth is like ten times more dirty than a dogs mouth? It's been scientifically proven…google it.

(BEAT)

No, really. You can google it on your phone right now. It's pretty gross stuff.

(BEAT)

Look. I'm sorry, Rebecca. I don't think this is going to work out. I just can't be with someone who double dips their chips. It's a huge pet-peeve.

(BEAT)

But, the night is not all ruined. You're at your favorite restaurant… and your Dad's here.

(BEAT)

Hey, go ahead and take the chips and queso to your Dad's table. It's on me. See you at school!

Originally performed by: Jake N. 2019. Platinum Award
Best Actor Award
Broadway Star Award

DOWN HOME
SOUTHERN COOKING

Hey, Ya'll!

Thanks for joining me here at Down Home Southern Cooking! It's a real pleasure to have you. You're probably saying, "Who is this girl and why is she on my television right now?" Well let me tell ya. My name is Rachel and I was approached by a couple of producers at the Clay County Fair. They had tried my award winning Apple Turnover Pie and after talking with me a bit, thought it would be worthwhile to give me my own show. So, here I am!

Well, enough about me, let's start cooking! Today, I thought it would only be fitting to make that Clay County Fair award winning Apple Turnover Pie! Now, I asked the producers to get me a few items from the store since I had to be at school all day and wouldn't have time to pick up the ingredients before our live program started today. That's right! We're live people!

As you can see we have fresh apples, cinnamon, sugar, flour, salt, and a few sticks of butter. Now, first thing you'll want to do is cut the apples into small...

(Tries to pick up an apple, but all the other apples come with it as the prop crew has glued them together)

What's going on here?...you know what? Let's just focus on the crust. Grab yourself a pinch of flour and...

(Tries to open flour and it is sealed shut)

This flour doesn't seem to want to cooperate. Let's just see if we can open the sugar.

(Sugar is sealed shut as well)

None of the ingredients that my producer got me today seem to be real.

(Grabs a stick of butter and it squishes in her hand)

Well, a majority of the ingredients.

(Wipes her hands on her apron)

Okay, ladies and gentlemen. I think we are going to have to postpone today's recipe for another time. I'm going to have to have a little chat with my producers about how actual, edible ingredients are needed in order to have a cooking show.

I hope ya'll had a good time and I can't wait to see you back in my kitchen for another episode of Down Home Southern Cooking!...If we haven't already been cancelled.

Originally performed by: Bianca P. 2019. High Gold Award

EMMA

(Walks up to the podium)

It was suggested that if I came up here and shared a memory of my sister that it might help me get through this difficult time.

(BEAT)

It's weird how memories work, you know? At the time when a memory is being made, it might seem like that moment is the worst moment of your life. Then, as you grow and learn more about life, you look back on some of those memories with fondness and laughter.

(BEAT)

When I was younger, I had this little rocking chair that I would always sit in when watching *Dora, The Explorer. Dora* was my favorite cartoon at that age. Every day I would sit in that chair and rock with my eyes glued to the television screen. Well, one day, after *Dora* was over, my sister Emma decided that we should play "Roller Coaster." This was easy for Emma because our living room was carpeted and she could scoot my little rocker with my little baby self in it without much resistance. We'd go all around the room. When the imaginary rollercoaster would go up, Emma would lean the chair back and I would scream with excitement. Then, when we would reach the top of the imaginary coaster and it was time to take that sudden drop, she would lean the chair forward. The thing about leaning the chair forward though was that I would always feel like I was going to fall out and I would put my feet out to touch the ground. Emma would say, "You've got to trust me, Parker. I won't let you fall." So, after about five dips on the rollercoaster track, I finally got the courage to keep my feet up. Emma leaned the chair forward and, for the first time, she let go of the chair. I don't think she meant to, it just kind of happened. I fell face first onto the ground. Emma screamed and quickly threw the chair off of me. My mother ran in the room frantically asking "what happened?" Emma quickly said that she didn't mean to let me go, her hands just slipped and the chair fell. As she was trying to explain what happened, I got up and turned around with a big smile on my face and said, "Sissy and I were playing rollercoaster!" I also had a lego stuck to my head, which after falling on, left a nice mark for about a week. I didn't feel any pain because I was having so much fun with Emma. She felt so bad afterwards. Mom told us we weren't allowed to play rollercoaster anymore after that.

(BEAT)

Emma always looked out for me. I will always be grateful for the time I was able to spend with her. I wish we had more time, but God had other plans. I'll always love you Emma, and I'll miss you every day until we are reunited again.

Thank you all for being here. It means a great deal to my family. Please remember to hug your loved ones hard. Let them know how much you love them. You never know if that might be the last time you can share that with them.

Originally performed by: Halle T. 2020. Platinum Award
Broadway Star

FLIRTY

Mr. Evans, can I ask you a question? What do boys look for in a girl? I'm asking because I have been trying to get Steven Door to notice me for weeks and have had zero results.

For instance, last week I was drinking water from the water fountain in the North Hallway when I saw Steven Door walking towards me as if he was in slow motion. So, I did what any girl in my situation would have done. I slowly raised my head from the drinking fountain, I shook my hair from side to side and batted my eyes right at him. He didn't even look at me. At that moment it felt like all of my life-force was rushing right out of me...but that was really only because I forgot to take my finger off of the water fountain's button, and as you know, the fountain in the North Hallway tends to overshoot. Needless to say, I walked around with a wet outfit the rest of the day.

Then, on Tuesday, I noticed that he didn't bring his lunch with him. So, I walked from my normal lunch table over to where he was sitting. I asked him, "Hey, Steven Door, I noticed you didn't have a lunch with you today. Would you like to share my turkey sandwich?" He looked up at me with those baby blue eyes. He opened his perfect mouth and he said, "Thanks, but I'm vegan this week." I was crushed...and impressed by his willpower. So, I just squirmed back to my lunch table and questioned every meal I've ever eaten.

Then, fifteen minutes ago in gym class, I decided "This is the time! Tell him! It's now or never!" So, I walked right up to Steven Door's perfect face and I said, "Steven Door, I LOVE YOU!" The entire gym went silent as I stood there with my arms stretched out, ready for his embrace. Ready for him to take me in his arms and say, "Kennedy, I've been waiting this entire year to hear those words from you! I love you too!" Just like in the movies, you know? But, all I heard was silence. When I opened my eyes, Steven Door was just standing there looking scared and frightened, like this *(she poses)*.

I'm all out of ideas Mr. Evans. Please help me find a way into Steven Doors heart!

(Silence)

Mr. Evans, why are you staring at me like that? You look just like Steven Door when I told him I loved him…You know what? I'm going to talk to Mrs. Kingsley. Maybe a woman's point of view will help me out of this predicament, since every male I've talked about this to so far just gives me this look… *(she poses)*. Goodbye, Mr. Evans.

OR ALTERNATIVE ENDING….

Mr. Evans, why are you staring at me like that? You look just like Steven Door when I told him I loved him…You know what? I'm going to talk to Mrs. Kingsley. Maybe a woman's point of view will help me out of this predicament. I mean, she's on her fourth marriage, so she must be doing something right. Right? Goodbye, Mr. Evans.

Originally performed by: Kennedy K. 2020. High Gold Award

FUNDRAISER

Mrs. Lindsay! Thank goodness I caught you before you left for the weekend! Ever since our class this morning, where you gave us the task of coming up with a fundraising idea, my brain won't let me think about anything else! So much so that I couldn't focus in Chemistry Class and I almost mixed oxidizing acids with rubbing alcohol!

(Laughs nervously)

That could have been a disaster...

Anyway, I have had so many ideas, but I've narrowed them down to three and wanted to run them by you.

(Opens notebook and papers fly everywhere)

Okay, my first idea is that we have everyone in our class bring in something that we can put into a themed basket. Like spa products, candy, or even rolls of cash. Everyone loves cash. It's a pretty simple fundraising idea and after researching it on the internet, it seems to work. The only problem is that it could be costly and do we really want to put all that money and time into baskets that someone might not even buy? And what about kids that don't get an allowance? They wouldn't be able to contribute as much and it might make them feel bad.

So, here's my second idea, you know when you go outside for a walk and as you are walking down the street you might see a flyer that catches your eye on a telephone pole? You say to yourself, "Oh, what's this? This flyer wasn't here yesterday. I wonder what it says?!. Wow! A fundraiser?! I love fundraisers! Why, I'll give twenty thousand dollars!!!" So, yeah, flyers could be a great option for our class. I've already did some preliminary sketches while I was in Geometry Class and they would look something like this.

(Pulls flyer out of notebook)

I'm sure we could reach a lot of the community who would want to give to us if we use flyers.

Now, onto my third, and final idea. We go to the pet store and purchase guinea pigs and then go to the craft store and purchase glitter. Everyone loves guinea pigs and everyone loves glitter…at least everyone I know. Once we have the guinea pigs, we get them wet and put glitter on their fur. Then we can sell them as exotic guinea pigs and make ten times what we bought them for!

Actually, saying my ideas out loud has really helped me realize that there is truly only one idea that will work for our class. So, I really need to get going. The pet store closes at six.

(Picks up all her papers that might have fallen)

See you Monday, Mrs. Lindsay!

Originally performed by: Sammie R. 2018. Platinum Award

GAMERS ANONYMOUS

(Sitting in a chair center stage)

I guess I'll go next.

Hello, my name is *(name)*. And I, like many of you, feel as if my family just doesn't understand me. I try to explain to them how their actions are impacting me, but my concerns seem to fall on deaf ears.

I can't tell you how very excited I was to stumble upon this group. It's such a relief to find like minded individuals who are experiencing the same occurrences. Karl, your story about getting lost in the forest and thinking you would never find a way out was heart wrenching. And Steve, after hearing your story and all that you went through for that princess, I can confidently say that she didn't deserve you.

My story starts like many of yours, I finally got my hands on a Sony Playstation 5 System. I rushed home and unpackaged the beautiful tower-like system that one could only dream about a few months earlier. Madden 21, the football game I had been waiting for, came as a bundle with the system. My hands were shaking as I was hooking the wires to their appropriate ports. I couldn't believe this day was finally here. It was one in the morning and the rest of my family was fast asleep. I knew there would be no slumber in store for me, so I started up the system. The graphics were beautiful. I felt fully immersed in the game. How many seconds, minutes, hours had I spent in front of the television? I couldn't tell you. All I know is that I found myself in the final quarter with five seconds left on the clock!

My team, the Jacksonville Jaguars, were down by two points and Josh Lambo *(or whoever is the kicker at this time)* was set up to kick the winning field goal.

My palms were sweaty, my eyes bloodshot from the lack of sleep. This was it! This was the moment. Finally, redemption for the Jags. The snap was called. Players scatter ready to protect the kicker. Just as I pressed the joystick on the controller forward, ready to clench the win for the Jags, my sons Joshua and Jacob came barreling into the room like two tornados wreaking havoc on everything in their path.

BAM!

I felt the controller get knocked from my hands. I watched as it spiraled to the ground. As I heard the plastic hit the floor, I looked up and saw that Lambo had kicked the ball and it was spinning toward the goal post. Those seconds felt like hours. The ball inching closer and closer with the potential of getting the points that we Jacksonvillian's needed to win the game. Then, after what seemed like days, a clunk was heard as the ball bounced off one of the goal posts and onto the soft grass in the end zone.

We lost the game.

As I stood there in shock and defeat, my wife walked in the room and said, "Oh good, you're awake before 6:30 for once. Could you please take out the trash?" She then kissed me on the cheek and left the room with a laundry basket.

I watched as my sons were now wrestling over the batman pez dispenser we got them for Christmas.

A single tear rolls down my cheek...

(Jokingly) Karl, I know that you know what I'm talking about! Thank you all for listening.

Originally performed by: Carter M. 2021

GIRL SCOUT COOKIES

Hello? Is anyone home? Hello?

(BEAT)

Oh! Hi there! Your front door was open, so I just let myself in. I hope you don't mind.

What a beautiful house you have! Oh! How rude of me. I haven't introduced myself yet. Hello, my name is Elizabeth and I represent girl scout troupe number 4431. You sure are looking great today if I do say so myself! You look like someone who really knows what they want in life and goes out to get those things without hesitation. It just so happens that I have something to sell that you might be interested in buying!

(She reaches behind her back and excitedly pulls out a tube of toothpaste)

BAM! That's right, I have this AMAZING tube of toothpaste for sale today. I like to keep my customers happy, so I have personally tried this specific toothpaste and look at how shiny and white my teeth are! Many tubes like this have been selling for twenty-five dollars a piece, but I am going to make you a deal today! For this beautiful tube of toothpaste, you will only have to pay the very low price of TWENTY DOLLARS!

(BEAT)

You look very shocked. I know the price is super low for such a product, but I don't want you to worry about me. I'll get by. I just enjoy bringing the savings to you, the customer, who probably couldn't find this deal on their own.

(BEAT)

Did you say overpriced?! I'm sorry you feel that way, but I can attest that this toothpaste has been tested. I assure you that it is the best product for the brushing of teeth that you could possibly find!

(BEAT)

Cookies? No, we don't sell cookies anymore. Now, we are trying to be more health conscious and help people have healthy, glowing, radiant teeth!

(BEAT)

Okay fine, you got me. I ate all the girl scout cookies while watching *Frozen (or your favorite movie)* and now I have to find a way to pay for them all! Could you please help me out? Every little bit helps. If you don't need toothpaste, I also have a pair of "like new" socks in my wagon outside. These socks are special. Normally a sock only has one hole in it to put your foot through. Well, these socks have TWO holes!

(BEAT)

No? Well, it was worth a try. I'll just let myself out...

Originally performed by: Alayna M. 2018. High Gold Award

HISTORY 101

Good afternoon class. Welcome to American History 101. My name is Mr. King and I am your professor for this course. Now, let's get started. Open your books to page twenty nine. Today we are going to be talking about the Market Crash of 1929…what a coincidence that this topic starts on page twenty nine. How delightful.

(Notices a student in the audience, can be a person you are auditioning for)

Now, before we get started, what is your name young man?

(If he answers, say) Mr. (HIS NAME),
(If he doesn't answer, say) Ah, can't remember your name today? That's alright.

I noticed that you are wearing jorts today Mr. (NAME/NO NAME). You might not know this, but jorts are now on the updated dress code violation list. I'm going to let it slide today, since it's the first day of class, but I will be crashing down on you the next time it happens…

…much like the market crashed in 1929. Where stock holders lost forty billion dollars. Can anyone tell me how much that would be today? Anyone? Just yell it out.

(Notices another student)

Young lady, I just saw you yawn. Am I boring you? I also noticed that you have not taken any notes since we started class. Participation is fifty percent of your grade. If you don't participate, you will fail...

...much like the banks failed in 1929. Where millions of Americans lost all of their life savings.

I see a large percentage of you have partaken in the schools coffee initiative to keep you awake during school hours. I suggest you also drink a glass of water per cup of coffee because coffee will dehydrate you...

...much like the Great Drought of 1930 dehydrated much of our food supply, killing crops and making it harder to find meals for your families.

All of these things led to the Great Depression, which is what many students have told me they go through after being in my class.

Now, I want to give you an idea of what the food might have looked and tasted like during the depression. So, grab your coffee, cover your jorts with a jacket, and let's head down to the cafeteria.

Originally performed by: Carter M. 2020. Platinum Award
Best Actor Award
Broadway Star Award

IMAGINARY FRIEND PARTY

Okay everyone, Jeremy will be here any moment! He has no idea that we are throwing him this surprise birthday party! Don't worry, I'll let you know when he gets here since he is my imaginary friend and you probably can't see him. Everyone hide!

(A few BEATS pass)

I wonder what's taking him so long? When I was walking here he was just a little bit behind me. Where could he be? Don't worry, I'll retrace my steps. First, we went to the candy store and were trying to decide if we wanted a KitKat or Snickers bar...of course the KitKat won. Then, we were skipping through the park. Jeremy just loves skipping through the park. I just don't understand where he could be. He was with me the whole time.

(Gasps)

I didn't hold his hand when we were about to cross the street at the crosswalk! I always hold his hand at the crosswalk! He must have been too scared to cross the street alone. I left my best friend on the street corner...

(They start sobbing and hugs the air next to them. After a moment of sobbing they realize that they have been leaning on Jeremy this entire time)

Jeremy! Oh, thank goodness! I thought you were gone forever! I'm so sorry for leaving you behind at the crosswalk. I was trying to get back to the house to surprise you for your birthday.

(BEAT)

What do you mean your birthday isn't until next month?

(BEAT)

That's perfect! Do you know what this means?

(Now talking to their parent)

Mom, now you have enough time to get the ingredients for a real cake. His favorite is pineapple upside-down cake. Oh, and we can go to the party store to pick up all sorts of fun decorations! This is going to be the best imaginary best friend party ever!

Originally performed by: Tatum M. 2019. Auditions

INVESTIGATOR

(Enters stage with a flashlight. Slowly looking around)

My Mom says that I can't be a paranormal investigator. I told her, "that's what the ghost's want!"

She's been against my investigations from the start. Like that time I broke into the Laughtry's house next-door because I saw a gnome glaring at me through their front window, taunting me. They claim it was Mrs. Laughtry practicing her dance routine for her upcoming performance at the senior center, but I knew better. When the police were escorting me back to my house, I tried to explain to them that we had to stop the gnomes or they would eat all of the Laughtry's socks. Old people can't just go out and buy all new socks, they're on a fixed income. But, the police officers wouldn't listen.

(BEAT)

Graveyards are my favorite, mostly because of the thrill. One moment you'll be walking one direction and you hear footsteps behind you, so you turn! There's nothing there and all you hear now is your own breathing. So, you start walking in another direction and you hear the footsteps again! So, you turn! Nothing there again. Then, as you are about to start walking again, you run into a big scary guy that says, "not you again, kid!" And you turn and run home as fast as you can!

Nothing is going to stop me from achieving my dreams! Not even being on house restriction. Which is why I am here in the basement searching for clues to the paranormal. So, if there are any ghosts or ghouls who want to chat, I'm listening.

(BEAT)

Okay, well, I'll be on house restriction for the next month because I tried to save the Laughtry's socks. If you want to talk, you know where to find me.

Originally performed by: Christian D. 2017. Platinum Award
Performed by: Mikayla (Mickey) T. 2018. High Gold Award

LIMITED TIME OFFER

(Bailey McGreen enters stage crying/wailing in an overdramatic way. This goes on for a bit until her head pops up and she says..)

Hi! I'm Bailey McGreen, world-renown actress and impersonator extraordinaire! Many people ask me, "Bailey McGreen, how do you act so darn good?" And I tell them the truth...

Acting *(poses)* is reacting *(reacting to first pose)*.

For instance, in "A Spy is Born," I had to look like I knew what was going on at all times. So, when someone said something smart, I would shake my head like this. *(Acts like she knows what is going on)*

Or, when I played Molly in *I Love You, You Horrible Person!* I had to pretend that I was in love with Nathan, the rug cleaning boy. "Nathan, put down that carpet cleaner, I love you!"

Or, when I played Abraham Lincoln in the historical piece, *This isn't Historically Accurate.*

(she slowly mimes putting on Abraham Lincoln's top hat)

"I'm Abraham Lincoln."

Acting, for me, is easy. Acting, for anyone else, is the MOST DIFFICULT THING EVER IMAGINABLE!

However, I have great news! Now you! YES, YOU! Can become a master of acting just like Bailey McGreen…when not "just like" Bailey McGreen, but you will at least learn how to act with a smidgen of the mastery that oozes from my pores. You'll learn how to portray amazing emotions like never before.

HAPPY! *(acts happy)*

Sad. *(acts sad)*

Angry! *(acts angry)*

Scared. *(acts scared)*

And Content. *(acts content)*

(Snaps)

That's acting! And now you have the chance to spend thirty minutes with me, learning how to use your acting skills to transport your audience to another world.

(Starts fanning herself)

Are we in Hawaii right now?…NO! That was just my acting talents! You don't want to miss out on this opportunity. Call now! Space is limited due to the fact that I am going on a cruise with myself next week.

Only five thousand dollars per spot! Don't wait! Reserve your spot today!

ACTING!

Originally performed by: Isabella W. 2018. Platinum Award

LOAF OF BREAD

(Falls onto stage as if being thrown)

No! Please! Please let me out! I only took that bread because my family was starving. We don't have any money. Come back! Please!

(Realizing the guards aren't coming back. Taking in the space. Trying to think of a way out. Then, overcome with grief)

Father, I know you can hear me. I know you're watching over us, but things are getting out of control. We've been trying to play by the rules, but it seems like everything is against us. Henry hasn't been able to keep a job and the landlord has really taken advantage of us since you left. Mother has been sick and we're afraid it's the same sickness that took you. I don't know what Henry or I will do if we lose her too.

The King doesn't care about us, he only cares if we can pay his taxes. We need a little help Father. I made a horrible mistake. Our family needed me and now I'm stuck in here for trying to find food to feed everyone. I should have stuck with something small like fruit, something easy to hide.

I'm sorry Father. I told you that I would look after everyone and I've let you down.

Please, give me a sign that you are here with me…

(BEAT)

Any sign…

(Nothing happens. They find an old blanket in the corner of the cell and, defeated, decide to wrap themselves in it. As they are wrapping themselves they hear a clang of metal. A spoon has fallen out of the blanket. They now have hope. They try to find a weak spot in the walls where the spoon might help dig their way out. They find one. First, they have small chunks coming off of the wall and soon entire rocks can be moved away. Once the hole is large enough, they can pull themselves through. On the other side of the cell they are relieved)

Thank you Father!

(Runs off stage)

Originally performed by: Abigail D. 2018. Platinum Award
Broadway Star Award

LOLA

Someone was in trouble, so I helped them out. Isn't that what you and Dad always tell me to do?

(BEAT)

That dog is a living thing too! I don't care if Mr. Avery is her owner. He leaves her outside on that chain all day and night. There is no shade for her to get out of the sun and yesterday she didn't even have any water in her bowl. So, yes, I jumped the fence into Mr. Avery's yard. I gave Lola some water and she still looked so sad. So, I took the chain off of her collar and for the first time, she seemed alive and free. She was running around and wanting to play. It was great Mom! She was running around me so fast that I got dizzy trying to watch her. When I got my balance back, I looked around and couldn't see where she had went. Apparently, she squeezed through where a loose board was in the fence and took off down the street. She's finally free Mom and hopefully she will find a family that will take care of her better than Mr. Avery! I'm sorry that I had to break the rules, Mom. I understand why I will be grounded, but I'm not ashamed of what I did. I truly believe that Lola is out there living a better life than what she had with Mr. Avery.

Originally performed by: Tatum M. 2019. Platinum Award
Broadway Star Award

LOVE AND FEAR

Mom, listen to yourself! You are the parent, not me. Why am I the one worried about if Tyler gets fed at night? Why am I the only one who cleans the house and washes the dishes and does the laundry? You just sit in your chair watching tv. I could understand if these were my chores, but we don't have chores in this house. I do all of these things because if I don't do them, they won't get done. You have to stop dreaming about what you do not have and start living with the stuff that is right in front of you. You have me. You have Tyler who was such a blessing, who has brought so much happiness to this family and who needs YOU! Nothing out there is going to give you the love that you will get from the people you have right in front of you. Please start taking responsibility. We need you Mom.

This is your chance to do something right. Something that can help all of us. You will finally get the help you need. Just sign the paper.

This isn't up for negotiation. Either you do this or I'm taking my brother and we are leaving.

You have to know that this is the best thing for you. Please sign the paper so we can get you help.

Okay, then. You've done what you thought you needed to do, and now I have to do what I know is right. I'll pack up Tyler's things and we'll be on our way.

I wish you would have chosen us for once.

MADAM CYNTHIA

(Madam Cynthia enters the space chanting and waving her arms almost as if dancing. Once she gets to the center of the space, she stops, notices all the people around her, smiles and says...)

Why, hello there everyone! Welcome to Madam Cynthia's Fortune Telling *(said to the side)* and tax auditing *(back to normal)* services. I am, of course, Madam Cynthia.

(Looking around at the audience)

My, there are so many of you who have come to ask questions of Madam Cynthia.

(She goes into a trance and then finds a woman in the audience)

Ah, yes. You, Ma'am. You have a question for Madam Cynthia. Yes! I can hear this question very clearly in my mind. You would like to know... what color eyeshadow to wear to catch the eye of the man sitting next to you?

(Looking at the man next to woman)

Yes, you sir!

(She winks at him then waves her arms and goes into another trance)

Yes, YES! It's becoming clear. He likes bright colors!

(Quickly shifts out of the trance and talks directly to the woman as if she were a friend)

I would go with the NYX Professional Make-up Brights Ultimate Shadow Palette. My sister uses it and now she's married to a very wealthy husband.

(She goes back into the trance)

Yes, I hear someone else who has a question. It's coming from this side of the room. It's so clear. And the answer to your question is yes, YES! Yes, everyone IS judging you for eating fish in an enclosed area.

(BEAT)

OHHHH! I'm hearing another question. This one is very strong. It's coming from right over here. It's from a parent. They're wondering… is this child's monologue…ever going to end?

(Comes out of the trance)

The answer is yes, very soon!

(Back to her normal self)

Thank you all for visiting Madam Cynthia's Fortune Telling…and tax auditing…Services. There is only one way out of this room, and it is through my cash register. So, collect all of your belongings and follow me. I accept cash, check, Cashapp, PayPal, and Venmo. Right this way.

Originally performed by: Isabella W. 2018. Platinum Award

MELODY

(They walk on stage with a flower, looking through gravestones until they find the one they were looking for. They sit down next to the gravestone, pull out a book, and begins to read)

"Melody was righteous and honorable and true,
Those monsters didn't know what to do.
She opened her heart for all that could hear,
There was no longer anything for you to fear.
The light of her love sent the monsters away,
But, there was a price for this that she would pay.
Her passion to fight helped her family through,
Melody was righteous and honorable and true."

I finally finished our book, Mom. It took me a long time to even look at if after you…after you left us, but it's finally complete! I haven't shown anyone yet, not even Dad. You were the first person I wanted to share it with.

When you passed on, it was hard to even look at the poems that we wrote together. I was so angry that you were no longer here with us. I did and said things that I'm not very proud of. I threw some of the poems in the garbage out of anger, I didn't think of how much I might treasure them later once some of the pain had subsided. Luckily, Dad found them in the garbage and saved them in a box for me. We were cleaning out the extra room and I found them. I cried so much because I was so happy they weren't lost forever. I took it as a sign that you wanted me to continue writing. I took some of the poems we wrote together and some of my new ones and put them into this book. We're published, Mom!

I asked Dad to stay in the car so I could share the book with you first. He knows how important this was to both of us.

Oh, this is your copy. The book's dedicated to you.

I love you, Mom. I miss you every day and I hope this book will keep you company until the day we can be together again. Until then, I'll keep writing knowing that you are watching over me.

Originally performed by: Ciara W. 2018. High Gold Award

MOM'S PRESENTATION

I know that we were supposed to do a presentation today about things that we like, but one thing that I really don't like is getting up in front of people and talking about myself. So, Miss Kelly, since there weren't any rules against doing our presentations as someone else, I will be giving my presentation today as....my mother.

(Takes a second to get into character)

(As Mother) Hello students of Miss Kelly's class! My beautiful daughter Hailey, *(to Hailey)* Hi sweetheart!

(Runs into the audience and sits down)

(As Hailey) Mom, you're embarrassing me!

(Runs back onto stage. As Mother) Isn't she just the cutest? My beautiful daughter Hailey has asked me to come into class today to talk about one of her favorite things. Let me start off by saying that as a child she was always into squishy, gooey materials. At halloween, as we would carve pumpkins, her favorite part would always be taking out their guts and squishing them in her hands. So, it only makes sense that she would grow up to enjoy the feel of cold, squishy, gooey slime.

It all started one fateful morning last March when my beautiful Hailey stumbled upon Talia Tossle's youtube video on how to make the perfect slime. As my carpet, couch, and glue filled laundry room sink can attest, making slime has become a passion of Hailey's ever since that fateful day. Some might even say, it's become an obsession. But, she is not alone. Did you know that girls of all ages now give out slime as party gifts? Bottles of glue are sought after like jewelry and there are entire shopping aisles dedicated to slime making products. It's quite an industry.

My Hailey has even become more inquisitive now. Every day I hear questions such as, "Which slime is your favorite?" and "Is this texture correct?" and "Do we have any more blue food coloring?" To which I respond, "Hailey, I am on a ZOOM meeting for work, can't this wait?"

In the end though, I am happy to endure the multiple trips to Michael's, the many slime related questions, and constantly using the plunger on my laundry room sink. You may ask, "but, why?" And the answer would be because Hailey is learning. Learning science through play, learning how to clean up after herself, and most importantly, learning more about who she really is. A beautiful, amazing, talented, perfect...

(Runs into audience)

(As Hailey) MOOOOOOOOOOM!!!!!!

(Runs back on stage)

(As Mother) Sorry, Sweetie!

In conclusion, I am so happy that my daughter has found this amazing outlet because it has helped her become a smarter, more creative, and well rounded individual. I couldn't be more proud of her. *(BEAT)* Now I must be getting back to work. Please welcome Hailey back to the front of the classroom.

(Runs into audience. Hailey gets up and walks to front of class)

I hope you enjoyed my presentation. My mom can be a little embarrassing sometimes. Thank you.

Originally performed by: Kennedy F. 2021.

NEVER STOP BELIEVING

After the play was over, I quickly got out of costume and went out to see my family and friends. My adrenaline was still pumping from putting on the show. It was my first play ever and I said every single one of my lines correctly. I opened the door to the lobby and the first faces I saw were my Mom and Dad's. They were just as excited as I was. It was the first time in a while that the whole family was in the same place at the same time. Aunt Edna even got me flowers. This is something that I had been wanting to do for such a long time and I was so happy that everyone was able to get together to watch the show.

Everyone told me how proud they were of me and how good the show was. We all decided to go out to a late dinner at a restaurant down the street. Mom and Dad said they would pull the car around and pick me up once I was done making sure my backstage area was cleaned and ready to go for the show the next day. I started walking to the lobby door that led to back stage. I noticed that three eighth graders were standing next to the door. I assumed they were waiting on one their friends backstage, so I didn't think much of it.

When I got to the door and reached for the door handle, the tallest of the three boys stood in front of it.

"Look who it is! It's the star of the show! Can I have your autograph?" He said with in a teasing way. "Did you see all of the fans he had?! He's got to be famous!"

I told him I really needed to get backstage so I could make sure everything is together for the show tomorrow.

"So, you do think you're a star? Huh?" Before I knew it, the other two boys had grabbed my arms and the taller boy punched me in my stomach. "You think you're better than us?" Another punch to the stomach. The other two boys were laughing. "You're just some kind of dork who wants attention!" The two boys threw me to the ground as I struggled to catch my breath from being punched. As they were walking out, the tallest boy turned and said, "You'll never be cooler than us, just remember that." And they laughed as they exited through the side door of the theater.

(BEAT)

I didn't do any type of theatre the rest of the time I was in middle school. I had this fear that someone would always be waiting for me on the other side of a door, wanting to push me down, make me feel ashamed. We never figured out who those kids were…but that doesn't matter. I've learned something very valuable from them. They were so sad, scared, and angry on the inside that they thought making someone feel exactly the way they did would somehow make them feel better about themselves. They had won making me feel that way for a couple more years, but I was able to realize something. I am the only one who has the power over what I do, how I think, and what dreams I want to accomplish. It took some time, but I finally started performing again and it feels so good. I want to learn as much as possible and become a better actor. It's slightly to prove those guys wrong, but also because it's something that I really love doing and am getting pretty good at.

I actually feel sorry for them. That whatever they were going through was bad enough that they wanted to make someone else feel that pain. I hope they finally found peace in their lives. They tried to break me, but they only made me stronger, and I thank them for that. Never give up on your dreams, no matter how if other people might tell you that you won't achieve them.

Originally performed by: Kris S. 2019. High Gold Award

ONLINE FRENCH CLASS

I had my Mom sign me up for an online French class. I'm supposed to be part of a foreign exchange program next summer and I wanted to be as prepared as possible to communicate with the people of France. At first, it seemed like a great idea. There was a nice voice reading off new words and helping me through French sentence structure.

"I've got this", I told myself, "Easy Peazy!"

I didn't know how wrong I was. Before long, that nice soothing voice that was reading off new French words turned into a strict, demanding beast! It even stopped telling me what the new French words meant. I would just find myself in the middle of a long passage with new words that I've never heard before as the robot instructor would yell at me to decipher it or fail!
Of course it yelled in French, so I don't really know the extent of the threats it threw at me, but from it's tone I could tell it was frustrated.

You have no idea how stressful that can be until you're in the middle of it. The worst part is that this online course counts towards my GPA and it's too late to get out of it now! This could be the end of my future. My GPA may never recover! What college is going to take me if I fail something as simple as an online French course. It makes me wonder, are there students in France succumbing to the same fate as I? Are they being berated by a once kind and encouraging, but now a hard and strict authoritarian robot voice? Do they too fear for their academic future? Or were they taught English at an early age because the French believe in education, so they don't have to take classes from une professeur de robot pour apprendre à parler anglais?

(BEAT)

Wait…What did I just say? Did I just throw myself in the middle of a French passage without knowing what the words mean?

HAVE I BECOME UNE PROFESSEUR DE ROBOT?

(Shocked and then comes up with an idea.)

Now is probably a good time to take that test I've been putting off.

(BEAT)

Salut!

(BEAT, realizing and happy he spoke French again, then hurriedly exits.)

Originally performed by: Casey C. 2021.

PAGEANT

(Enter, yelling offstage) I'VE GOT IT MOM! EVERYTHING IS FINE!

(Does a breathing exercise to center herself. She then smiles and makes her way downstage in front of the "Pageant Judges")

Hello, kind fellows and lovely ladies! I am very pleased to perform for you today in this wonderful, luxurious conference room area. If chosen, I believe I would be the best Little Miss Southeast ever! No need to ask me any questions, I have already prepared all the most important questions and answers for you.

(Clears throat. She is becoming both characters as she asks and answers each question.)
Who's your idol? Raven Simone *(or any other celebrity you look up to)*

What's your favorite color? Sea Foam Blue because it reminds me of the beach and sea turtles.

If you could have one wish granted, what would it be? *(BEAT)* World Peace.

Now that we got that portion of the pageant out of the way, I would like to move on to the talent portion. My talent? Mind reading!

(Goes to someone in the audience) Ma'am/Sir think of a number between one and ten.

(BEAT)

Think harder! You've got to work with me here ma'am/sir.

(BEAT)

Okay, I'm seeing something. Yes, you're number is...

(Say any number you like. If the number is correct, take a bow. If the number is wrong, say, "She's/He's obviously rooting for someone else!")

You ma'am/sir. Think of an animal.

(BEAT)

Yes, I'm seeing this very clearly.

(To first person she talked to)

Take notice ma'am/sir! This is how you put an idea out into the world.

(Back to animal person)

Ma'am/sir, what noise does your animal make?

(Person makes animal noise)

You are correct! Give them a round of applause!

Now, I will do three different poses so you can take pictures of me in my dress.

(Poses, poses, poses)

Thank you for all that you do!

(Walks backwards, takes a deep breath, slouches, walks offstage.)

I NAILED IT MOM!

Originally performed by: Ciara W. 2018. Platinum Award
Performed by: Claire S. 2019. High Gold Award

PLAY PRACTICE

Oh Leslie! I am so glad that we have become such good friends! And…I am so proud of you for getting on the cheerleading team.

(Does a cheer pose)

GO LIONS!

You're such a great person and I think for the rest of our lives, we're going to be the best of friends! You really mean the world to me.

(BEAT. Leslie is asking when your "Play Practice" is.)

When is my…"play practice?" Leslie, I don't have "play practice." I have "rehearsal." That's the correct verbiage. "Rehearsal," not "practice." I have rehearsal right after school until six. Also, I'm not rehearsing a play, it's a musical.

(Strikes a pose as she says the title of the musical)

"No Pickles on the Chic-Fil-A Sandwich Please!"

It's a new musical written by our drama teacher Mr. Franklin. I thought you knew the difference between a musical and a play. Here, let me explain. A musical has music and dancing. Plays on the other hand don't have music or dancing. Though there are some plays that do have music, but it's not enough music to be considered a musical. The play has to consist of at least sixty percent music and dancing to be considered a musical…I think that's right…I can't remember the specifics, but it's around that percentage.

(BEAT)

That look on your face makes me feel like you're still not understanding the difference.

(Upset)

I thought we had a deeper connection than just girls in a(n) *(Elementary/Middle/High)* school environment. But, if you can't distinguish the difference between a play and a musical, I'm not sure that I've ever really known you at all! And, I'm not sure if I want you to come see me in my first staring role in…

(Poses)

"No Pickles on the Chic-Fil-A Sandwich Please!" either!

(BEAT. Very sad and overdramatic)

I wish it didn't have to be this way Leslie, but you've given me no choice.

(BEAT)

Goodbye Leslie, may your remaining days be blessed with the bliss of your ignorance.

Originally performed by: Claire S. 2019. Platinum Award

PREPARING FOR A PET

(Child walks in with a dog puppet on their hand)

SIT!

(Dog puppet sits in child's arms)

My Mom told me that I had to prepare for when we pick up our new dog Chico tomorrow.

(As puppet) So, Keegan pulled me out of the toy box to practice for the new puppy.

(As Himself) That's right Bobo

(Quickly and excited as Dog) My name's Bobo!

(As Himself) He's Very Excited.

(As Bobo) So very Excited!

(As Himself) We want to make sure that Chico has a great, safe place to call home. First we checked the yard for any dangers and to see if there was any place where Chico might be able to get out.

(As Bobo) There were four holes in the fence that I got stuck in!

(As Himself) I didn't think I was going to get Bobo out of the last

one. His fabric got stuck on a large splinter

(*As Bobo*) I thought I was a goner! But, Keegan gently released me from my impending, splintery doom!

(*As himself*) We boarded up all the holes with extra plywood that we found in my Dad's shed!

(*As Bobo*) I held the hammer!

(*As himself*) Once Bobo was certain the fence was safe, we decided to move indoors. We wanted to make sure Chico couldn't get to anything that might break.

(*As Bobo*) So, Keegan strapped me to the top of a remote control car and crashed me into anything Chico might run into!

(*As himself*) Mom didn't like that too much, so we only secured the living room before she stopped us.

(*As Bobo*) I lost one of my eyeballs, but Keegan used some fabric glue he found in the art supplies box to glue it back on.

(*As himself*) And Finally, we tried to figure out how to potty train.

(*As Bobo*) Unfortunately, I don't have any organs, so Keegan is going to have to figure that one out on his own once Chico gets here.

(*As himself*) Yeah. (*looking a little worried about it*)

(*As Bobo trying to console Keegan*) It's probably for the best though! If I did have organs then you would have had to take me to the vet last night after I jumped up and ate all your chocolate.

(*As himself*) Yeah, that wasn't cool.

(*As Bobo*) My job is to act like a real dog. I'm pretty sure a real dog is going to want to share your chocolate.

(*As himself*) You're right.

(*As Bobo*) Umm...Keegan, when Chico gets here, you're not going to forget about me again are you?

(As himself) Forget about you? How could I do that? You've helped me so much in getting ready for Chico to get here! You're the reason I'm going to be prepared for him!

(As Bobo) I'm so happy that I could help!

(As himself) Plus, I think Chico would love to play with you!

(As Bobo) I can't wait to meet him!!! Though you better have that fabric glue ready. I have a feeling I might lose an eye or two.

(As himself) Do you think we've prepared enough for Chico's arrival?

(As Bobo) Well, I read on google that dogs also like to chew on things. Maybe we should check if there are any vulnerable, chewable surfaces that Chico would be able to get to.

(As himself) That's a great idea! Let's go!

(As he is exiting) Wait...how did you get on google?

(Exit)

Originally performed by: Keegan C. 2021

PUSHED

Why are you laughing? This isn't funny. It's not a funny matter. Do you normally laugh at people who come to you for help? The situation might not seem like a big deal to you, but let me make myself perfectly clear, it was degrading, terrible, and made me feel hopeless in a place where I'm supposed to feel safe. It wasn't horseplay Mr. Grimes. When they twisted my arm behind my back and pushed me to the ground, I wasn't thinking, "Oh, these kids are just having a little fun at my expense." When they held my face down on the pavement with their foot, I didn't say to myself, "Oh, this is just in good fun."

(BEAT)

I felt helpless Mr. Grimes. I was thinking, "where are all the people that are supposed to be helping me? Where are the people who are supposed to make sure there is no bullying going on? Where are my friends? Where are the teachers? Where is the Principal?" None of you were around.

This isn't the first time these bullies have harassed me. I've done everything that you're supposed to do when dealing with bullies. I've tried to ignore them. I've told my teachers about what they've been doing. I've tried to be their friend and all I got back was getting picked on even more. All I want is to be left alone. This is unacceptable and I'm not going to stand by and let this happen to another person in this school. If you aren't going to stand up for what's right, I will, no matter what the consequences are. I will not be silent, I will not stand on the sidelines like you. I will always do what is right. Because it seems that at this school, everyone is okay with what these bullies are doing as long as it doesn't affect someone they love. You have a daughter who goes here. How would you like it if someone held her face to the ground? I'm no longer going to be a victim, Mr. Grimes. I expect you to stand up and change how this school is dealing with these bullies. When I get home, I'm going to be writing the school board to let them know exactly what's been going on here and make sure they hold you accountable to start a change at this school. You need to take this seriously, teach your staff how to identify these problems early so that this bullying doesn't lead to something much worse that you can't just fix with a, "kids will be kids" speech.

Do Better!

Originally performed by: Isabella W. 2018. High Gold Award

RIGHT THING TO DO

I know it was the right thing to do, reporting it, but I don't think she will ever forgive me. My sister hasn't coped very well since Mom and Dad passed away last year. I've had to be the strong one. I've tried to help her, get her into a clinic at least. They never did anything to help her though. Every clinic has said, "if she doesn't want treatment, there is nothing we can do." She's an addict. She doesn't know what she truly wants anymore because she has this addiction. We used to go bowling, to the beach, to our favorite sub shop *The Bread Oven.* She would always get the turkey bacon on a wheat roll and I would get the Italian. We would hang out together all day.

Now the only interaction I have with her is over the phone when she needs money. Once, I hadn't seen or heard from her in three months and then, as I'm walking home from school, I get punched in the arm and it's Elizabeth walking next to me with a stolen iPad and Apple Watch.

She's not the same person she was a year ago. This might be the last chance she has to get back to a normal life. Please, I'm begging you, keep her here. You say that she's been improving, if you let her go there's a good chance she will just jump right back into the addiction. We need to get her the help she needs now, even if she doesn't want it. Even if she fights tooth and nail, she needs to stay here. I need my sister back and I'm afraid if you let her go there won't be another chance to save her. Please, help me save my sister.

Originally performed by: Mallorie S. 2018. Platinum Award

SLIME

Mom! I just saw the most amazing thing! I was flipping though the channels on our TV when, out of no where, Nickelodeon hits me with all the feels. There is a new show coming on this summer. In this show, contestants compete in pairs and win prizes by doing challenges, going through obstacle courses, and answering trivia questions. We have to get on this show Mom! I'll even agree to let Henry, your son and my annoying brother, be my teammate. I know, Henry and I don't get along very often, but I'm willing to make that sacrifice in order to bring honor to our family. Because, Mom, THEY HAVE SLIME! They have gallons and gallons of slime that they pour on the contestants! SLIME, MOM! Can you imagine feeling the soothing, cool, refreshing slime all over your body? Mom, you know how much I love slime. It's a stress reliever when Henry does something dumb like, chew with his mouth open. Or, when he says, "Good Morning" to me when I see him in the morning. Or, how he answers the phone with "Hello!" Ugh, he get's on my nerves so bad that...

(To calm themselves down, they grab a tub of slime and squeeze it in their hands. This slowly calms them down and now they are in a zen type state as they say...)

So, Mom. We have to get on this show. I'm going to start making t-shirts because we are going to need to send in an audition video. I need you to get the contact information for Nickelodeon and then utilize your aggressive Mom tricks that you use with the teachers at school to get us in front of the producers. Double Dare isn't going to know what hit it!

Originally performed by: Ari W. 2019. Platinum Award

SPORTS

Look, Dad. I'm not great at sports. I never have been and I probably never will be no matter how many teams you sign me up for. Do you think I like being out there in front of everyone, failing week after week? Do you think it's fun for me in the locker room after the game, being looked down on by the other players? No, it's not. I understand you want me to meet new people and make new friends, but sports aren't the way for me to do that. We've done it your way. I've tried as hard as I could at each sport I've been a part of. Now, I would like to try it my way. Please. Can I please try out for the spring play at school? You always tell me I'm funny and that I have a knack for keeping people entertained. This may be something that I'm actually good at. I just need a chance to try. If I fail, I fail. I'm not afraid of failing. I've failed at so many other things…but this is something that I've been wanting to do for a long time. So, please Dad. Do I have your permission to audition for the spring play?

Originally performed by: Christian D. 2017. Platinum Award
Performed by: Keegan C. 2023. Auditions

SPRINKLES

(On stage there is an easel with poster boards on it)

Good afternoon fellow classmates. As you know, today we were tasked with bringing in a presentation on the thing that we love the most in life. Most of you brought in presentations about your pets or your parents. And even though I love both of those things, I've decided to do my report on something else that I love.

(Flips first poster board)

Rainbow Sprinkles! And here are the many reasons why they are the love of my live!

(Flips poster board)

Number 1: They are colorful and fun. No matter what your favorite color is, you will find it in a Rainbow Sprinkle. You like red? They've got red. You like yellow? They have yellow! You like blue? They have seventeen different shades of blue! I've counted. I made my Mom take me to six different stores yesterday to count. She also bought me four new containers of neon colored stars…which brings me to my next point.

(Flips poster board)

Number 2: Rainbow Sprinkles come in many different shapes and forms. You want a cupcake to reflect your favorite animal? BAM! You can get sprinkles that are in the shape of a turtle. You want to celebrate seeing a rainbow? BAM! There is a sprinkle rainbow on your cake! You want to be reminded of your favorite late 90's early 2000's girl group? BAM! Spice Girls Sprinkles on your pancakes! That one was for you Mrs. Holly. "Sprinkle up your life!" Side note, I'm not making it up. They actually do have Spice girl Rainbow Sprinkles.

(Flips poster board)

And now, my third and final reason as to why I love Rainbow Sprinkles so much. They represent me! They're colorful, they're bright, they're fun, and they make everything you put them on better. All of which brilliantly describes me to a "T". Colorful, bright, fun, and I make everything better.

In conclusion, Rainbow Sprinkles are by far the best thing ever created. Any party would be lackluster without these colorful, fun shaped, delicious morsels. Just like any party would be lackluster without me.

(Looks at a student in the class)

That's directed at you Gena. I saw you handing out invites to your thirteenth birthday party yesterday. You don't want it to be a bust do you? I didn't think so!

(Back to presentation)

Classmates, thank you for your time and good luck with topping that! Get it?…Because you top things with Rainbow Sprinkles?

Okay, Mrs. Holly, I'm done now.

Originally performed by: Reagan T. 2020. Platinum Award
All Star Actor Award

STORY TIME

Hello, class!

(BEAT)

I SAID, Hello, class!

That's much better. Thank you all so much for welcoming me into your classroom today. Your teacher, Mrs. Fuller, has been such an inspiration to me and I really want to make her proud. So, today I have a very special treat for you. We're going to be reading a story that my boyfriend, Chad, wrote for me to read to you today. Chad has been very supportive of my choice to become a teacher and he wanted to help out in any way he could. Isn't that the sweetest thing you've ever heard?

(BEAT)

I said, Isn't that the sweetest thing you've ever heard?!

(Audience responds)

That's what I said! Okay, the book he wrote is called, "The Sword and the Rock." Are you guys excited?

ARE YOU GUYS EXCITED?

(Audience responds) Oh, wonderful! Let's get started.

(Opens books, realizes children aren't sitting correctly)

Oh, everyone, criss cross applesauce if you are sitting on the floor. Those of you big boys and girls in chairs, make sure your feet are hanging down to the ground and your hands are in your lap. Little girl, that means you as well. Please get off your phone. I don't know why you would need a phone in kindergarten. Now, let's begin. "Once upon a time, there was a…"

(Notices little girl picking her nose)

Little girl! Please stop picking your nose. Remember, hands in lap. Okay, let's continue. "Once upon a time, there was a sword, and next to that sword…"

(Notices student starting to fall asleep)

Hey!..Hey you!…Little boy! *(Snaps fingers at child)* Little boy, I'm reading you a story. This is not the time to sleep. That's very rude. Would you like it if I fell asleep while you were trying to ask me a question? No, I wouldn't think so. So, please, let's get through the story that Chad, my boyfriend, has written for us today. Okay? Okay.

"Once upon a time, there was a sword and next to this sword was a rock."

(Turns page)

"The End"…wait…

(They turn through the pages trying to find more of the story, there is none. They are horrible disappointed with Chad.)

Well, I hope you enjoyed our story time as much as I did today children. This isn't exactly how I dreamed my first day co-teaching would go, but at least now I know how helpful and committed Chad, my soon to be ex-boyfriend, really is. Have a great day students!

Originally performed by: Mallorie S. 2017. Platinum Award
Performed by: Bella D. 2018. High Gold Award
Performed by Haley S. 2019. High Gold Award

SUNSHINE GIRL

I study a lot. I get good grades. I raise my hand in class to answer questions. I've always done this because I believe it is important to try to become the best version of yourself that you can be. The more you research things, the more you can understand the world around you, how it works, and the people in it. I also know that around school I am known as the bubbly girl. The girl who is always smiling. "Oh, there goes the ray of sunshine girl, happily skipping down the hallway!" I hear all the jokes and comments people make about me. Typically, I let it roll off my back. They don't know me, they don't know the hardships I've been through and on the opposite side, I don't know what they've been through either. So, I alway choose to be kind and generous to everyone, even if they don't treat me with the same kindness or generosity. I expect the comments from them. I expect the jokes from them.

(BEAT)

I've noticed that you have started hanging out with these popular kids, and in turn, have been spending less time with me. I've seen how you try to dodge me in the hallway. I let all of that go though because you are my best friend. I thought you might be going through something, so I decide to give you some space. But then, this morning, you walked right past me and I heard you audibly repeating the same things that these "popular" kids have been saying about me. The same words that I told you hurt me, you used to describe me. My best friend, making fun of me.

You've changed Rebecca and it's not a good change. You decided to give up a true friendship for popularity. I hope they accept you for all your flaws, like I did. I hope they stand by your side and protect you, like I did. And I hope they are more kind to you than the previous girls that you are now replacing in their clique.

I'm going to go on with my life treating people with decency and respect. Trying to make their lives a little more brighter by showing kindness and being my happy, bubbly self. God knows we need a little more brightness in this cruel world. I wish you the best Rebecca, I really do. Thank you for teaching me a valuable lesson. As you go on with your new friends, I hope they don't crush your heart the way you've destroyed mine.

Originally performed by: Reagan T. 2020. Platinum Award
All Star Award
Best Actor Award
Broadway Star Award

THEATRE ETIQUETTE

(Storms onto the stage)

Mrs. Cornwall, I regret to inform you that someone was not following proper theatre etiquette rules during the first act of our productions of *"Les Miserable...In Space."* You've had this discussion with the entire cast at least one hundred times and still, when I came offstage to grab my laser gun, it was not in it's place. Someone moved it Mrs. Cornwall!

"If it's not your prop, don't touch it!" Isn't that the number one rule in theatre? Isn't that the one rule that you try to instill into our brilliant, but scattered, young actor's brains Mrs. Cornwall?

The top two suspects are Jenny Carrington and Sam Kinney. Those are the only two people who would have motivation to do something so horrendous! Jenny Carrington has had it out for me ever since she thought I tripped her on stage in our last show *"Rent...A Car!"* And Sam Kinney told me he had a crush on me last year and I had to turn him down because I am trying to focus on my career at the moment. If it was him, I'm sure he has hidden my prop in a place where I will be forced to talk to him. I won't fall for his tricks though, Mrs. Cornwall.

The worst part of all of this is that I even took precautionary measures so that my props wouldn't be moved or touched by anyone! I put a piece of velcro on each and every one of my props so that they would stay securely on the prop table until I needed to use them.

Yes, I know that velcro isn't the quietest, but it was necessary to ensure that my props would stay secure…and now my trust of the theatre community here at Mae West's Baptist School of the Arts has been broken! It is extremely clear that someone has malicious intents to destroy this production. Act two should be starting any minute now, but I know that you will have this under control as we move on with this show. I expect this matter to be dealt with swiftly and with a heavy hand Mrs. Cornwall!

Enjoy Act Two!

(They turn and we see that their laser gun prop has be stuck to their back because of the velcro this whole time)

Originally performed by: Alayna M. 2020. Platinum Award

THE MOST AMAZING HAROLD

Hello and welcome!

Wow! This is such a great turn out! I knew my flyers would draw a crowd, but…wow!

(Calming himself down)

Okay Harold, pull it together.

(To audience)

Hello and welcome to *"The Most Amazing Harold's Magic Show!"* Presented in my garage on third street north. This show is free of charge to you the public, though we do graciously accept donations.

Now, without further ado, we start the show.

My first trick is a simple card trick. I need everyone in the audience to think about a card that would be in a normal deck of playing cards. Yes, everyone think hard. Okay, now open your eyes! Oh, wait. I forgot to tell you to close your eyes. That messes up the trick. So, everyone close your eyes! Okay, NOW think of a card that would be in a normal deck of playing cards. There we go, now, open your eyes! Is this anyone's card?!

(Pulls out a card. If someone says yes, then say "Really? This is your card?! AWESOME!" If no one says that this is their card, go through a couple more

cards and then clumsily drop the entire deck on the ground. Pick them up and put them away somewhere)

Thank you! Thank you! Onto my next trick. It is the old "Pull the rabbit out of the hat" trick.

(Grabs top hat, shows that there is nothing inside. He then puts his hand in the hat and pulls it out...nothing there. He tries a couple more times and cannot pull the rabbit out of the hat)

Seems like the rabbit has escaped. *(Jokingly)* If you see a white rabbit running around, please let me know. *(Seriously)* No, but seriously, that rabbit was my whole allowance for the month.

Anyway, moving on. For my final trick of the day, I will need the help of my beautiful assistant!

(Motions for assistant to come out on stage. No one comes out.)

I said, MY BEAUTIFUL ASSISTANT!

(No one comes out, Harold walks to side of stage whispers loudly)

Shelly, you're on!

Okay, well...looks like I'm on my own for this trick then...Okay.

(Walks over to a blanket that is on the ground near a wing of the stage)

The show must go on...so...I will now disappear right before your very eyes. This is a feat that has never been done without an assistant present before. So...here we go.

(Lifts blanket in front of him. Fabric is covering what he is doing. Shakes fabric a couple of times. Then, throws the blanket up and runs offstage.)

**(You can end the monologue here or if there is a backstage where you are performing the monologue, continue with the following...)*

(We hear Harold trying to get from one side of the stage to the other while running into obstacles.)

Rex, get out of the way you dumb dog! Ow! Why is this hallway filled with so many things?!

(Comes out on the other side of stage)

TADAAA!

(Bows)

I would like to thank you all for coming to see *"The Most Amazing Harold's Magic Show!"* If you are so inclined donations are to be made payable to Nancy King. That's my Mom and she's the only one with a bank account. Again, I'm The Most Amazing Harold and I thank you for coming to see my show!

Originally performed by: Dominic S. 2018. High Gold Award

THE FUNERAL

Hello everyone, thank you all for coming. I know many of you never got to meet Henry in the short time that he was with us, but I can tell you that he would have loved to see all of your faces here today. I wanted to say a few things before we said our last goodbyes. Henry was the best listener. No matter what, when I needed someone to lean on, he was there for me. He never judged or made me feel bad for anything that I said or that I was feeling. He really helped me through some hard times this year.

He was quite possibly the best swimmer I know. Swimming so many laps a day. I think swimming was his favorite things to do, besides eating. When dinnertime came around, you could just see the excitement in his little face.

Now, before we send him on his way, I wanted to share the last thing that Henry said to me.

(Turn out Henry is a fish. So, they mimic a fish's face and imitates blowing bubbles while saying "Bloop, bloop...bloop")

Okay, Mom. You can flush the toilet now and send Henry on his way.

(BEAT, looks at watch on wrist) Oh, Mom! If we hurry, we can make it to the pet store before it closes! I promise this time I'll feed the next Henry more often! Let's go!

Originally performed by: Catherine T. 2018. Platinum Award

90

TRAVEL STORIES

I love traveling. It's my favorite thing to do. Seeing new places, learning about different cultures, trying new foods. It's all just so exciting! My family and I took a trip to Paris and we got to go to the top of the Eiffel Tower. Did you know you can see most of Paris from there? I didn't realize it was that tall! I'm not good with heights though. Going up was fine, but coming back down was an adventure. If you've ever seen a cat that hates water being forced into a bathtub, that's kind of what I looked like as we were coming back down from the top of the Eiffel Tower.

Another great trip was skiing at Breckenridge Ski Lodge in Denver, which is apparently the best skiing location in the United States based on this guy Chuck who wouldn't stop talking about it while we were putting on our ski's. I was like "We're already here, you don't have to sell us on this place, Chuck." I'm sure if they put Chuck in a commercial for Breckenridge that they would sell out year round, even if they didn't have any snow.

Now, my favorite place that I have ever travelled to was Santorini Greece. It's one of the Cyclades Islands in the Aegean Sea. Such an amazing place! Every beach was made up of lava pebbles that were either red, black, or white. I've never seen such a beautiful place. The thing that made this trip so special was that I was able to bring along a friend!

Abby is my best friend and we do everything together, so being able to invite her on a family vacation was amazing! First thing we did was collect some of the colored rocks on the beach near our hotel. Abby thought she had found a really cool looking rock and quickly realized she was mistaken when the crab latched onto her finger. We both yelled as she slung it into the water.

Next the whole family went on a trail up a volcano...you heard that right, we got to climb up a volcano! On the way up, Abby tripped on a rock and got her other foot stuck in a hole, which is how she got the tiny scar you can see on her knee. She will tell you that she fell into the volcano and we had to pull her out of it, saving her from falling to her "impending doom!" Sometimes she can be overdramatic, but I go with it for the sake of an awesome story.

On our final day in Santorini, my Dad was talking about these hot springs that were right near the volcano, but you had to take a boat to get to. He got us really excited to go and sit in the warm jacuzzi-like water. We all got into a boat and headed out to where my Dad said the springs were supposed to be. Once we got there, Abby and I were so excited. We all had on our life vests and Dad said, "Go ahead and jump in. We'll join you once we make sure the boat is securely anchored." So, smiling, Abby and I held hands, counted to three, and jumped. IT WAS THE COLDEST WATER I HAVE EVER BEEN IN! My father had really pulled one over on us. He did feel bad after we got back in the boat, body shivering and teeth chattering, so he took us back to the island and got us each a Saganaki. Which is a delicious snack of fried cheese in filo pastry covered in honey.

Overall, I'm just so glad that I could spend time traveling with my family and my best friend. Not to mention we have had some of the best over exaggerated stories to tell our friends back at school!

Originally performed by: Samantha G. 2021.

TRYOUTS

(Enters and starts stretching, then does a breathing exercise.)

Okay, I'm ready. I brought my headshot and sports resume, which I will give you at the end of my tryout. I wasn't sure what a sports resume would look like, so I just copied the format off of my acting resume. I don't want to waste your time, so I will go ahead and get started.

First, when calling the plays on the field, it is best to have someone who can project. So, I would like to demonstrate how well I can do that.

(Turns and walks to the back of the stage, turns to address the coaches and in a loud voice says...)

Okay, I'm ready! HELLO, BOY TO THE LEFT. I SHALL GIVE YOU THE BALL ONCE YOU RUN INTO THE CENTER OF THE FIELD. SIR TO THE RIGHT, PLEASE BLOCK ALL WHO LOOK LIKE MIGHT DO ME HARM FOR I HAVE BRITTLE BONES AND AM AFRAID OF CONFRONTATION! BLUE 42, BLUE 42, HIKE!

(Runs to the center of the stage and bows)

Thank you! Many years of practice PROJECTING in the theatre have given me this amazing foghorn instrument. Now, I would like to show you how nimble I am on my feet.

(CHOOSE ONE OF THE FOLLOWING)

(Pulls tutu out of his backpack and puts it on)

I shall now perform a ballet number for you.

(Performs it horribly)

(OR)

(Pulls soft foam balls out of his backpack and hands them to the "coaches")

Would you please throw these balls at me. As you can see, they are very soft and wouldn't be able to hurt anyone. This is just a demonstration.

(Coaches throw the balls and he dodges them as well as he can.)

Wow! You're really good at throwing. I'm surprised you didn't go to the major leagues!

(CONTINUE FROM HERE)

The last thing I will be showing you today is probably the most important thing of all sports games. The pose that I will be doing for my sports cards. Since I am not sure what sport I am auditioning for today, I shall do them all for you.

(Does a different pose for each sport)

This is my baseball card pose. This, my football. Hockey, soccer, tennis, table tennis, and of course, bocce ball.

Now, I am sure you have other people to audition today, so I will take my leave. My name is *(Your Name)* and I want to thank you for this opportunity to tryout for your sports team, whatever sport it may be.

Originally performed by: Luke G. 2017. Platinum Award
Broadway Star Award
Performed by: Ari W. 2018. Platinum Award
Broadway Star Award
Performed by: Keegan C. 2023 High Gold Award

TWINS
(Mature Content)

When we got there, the guards opened the doors and pushed everyone out of the train car. I remember my twin brother Matthew and I clinging to my mother's side. Everyone was pushing and shoving trying to get out. At one point, I lost my grip on my mother's dress and I fell down. By the time I got back up, there was a sea of people moving every which way and I couldn't find her. I yelled for her as I pushed through the never-ending wall of people. Finally, after what seemed like hours, I heard her frantic voice calling back. I saw her worried face and I ran as fast as I could to get back to her.

(BEAT)

I wish I hadn't yelled at all. It drew attention to us. One of the guards yelled "Zwilling!" Which is German for "twins." Before we knew it, both Mathew and I were scooped up and separated from our mother. We yelled and fought to get back to her. The last thing a remember was being hit and blacking out. That was the last time either of us saw our mother.

(BEAT)

Twins are important to them. They run a lot of tests to see how we work, how alike or different we are.

(BEAT)

They took Matthew yesterday morning for more testing and he hasn't been back yet. Normally when people are taken and don't return in the same day, the don't come back.
(BEAT)

He's all I have left in this world. What if one of the tests didn't go as they had hoped and he didn't make it through? Did they just throw his body with the others who were killed before him? Are they coming to run the same tests on me to see how my body reacts? If Matthew is gone, then I might no longer be of any use to them. It's been one hundred and sixty seven days since we got to the camps. I don't know how many more days I have left. The only comfort that I have is that whatever happens, eventually I will be reunited with my family on the other side. I have to endure this torture until that day arrives.

Originally performed by: Catherine T. 2019. High Gold Award

VISITING HOURS

(Leah enters into her Grandmother's room at an assisted living facility)

Hey Grandma! Your favorite Granddaughter is here! I brought you some dark chocolate and licorice, because I know it's your favorite. I even brought you a new picture of Jason, he's getting so big! I'm sure Mom will bring him by soon.

(BEAT. Grandma seems to not remember who Leah is.)

Oh…I'm Leah. I'm your Granddaughter. I try to come by at least two times a week to see you. It's not a good day today, huh? Don't worry though, I'll help you through it. Let's look at some of the pictures in our picture book and see if we can spark some good memories.

(She pulls out the book)

Let's see. Oh, this is Helen, she's your daughter and also my mother. That man standing next to her is Kevin. He's her husband and my father. It took you a long time to accept Dad as family because you though he wasn't good enough for Mom because you didn't think anyone was good enough for Mom. She's a pretty awesome individual and, if I do say so myself, I think she made the right choice in Dad.

Oh, here is when we all went to Disney World together. We all got ice cream bars shaped like Mickey Mouse. We laughed a lot that day. This was our last family vacation before you started losing your memory.

(BEAT)

It's okay Grandma! It's okay not to remember. Some days are good days and some days are not so good, but we will always be there for one another because we're family.

(BEAT)

You know what? I'm going to give Mom a call and let her know I'll be staying a little longer with you today. Okay? Everything is going to be fine Grandma. I also think I saw some cookies in the cafeteria on my way to your room. So, I'll pick up a couple of those and we can eat them while we look through some more photos in our picture book.

I love you Grandma. I'll be right back.

Originally performed by: Ashley G. 2017. High Gold Award
Performed by: Bella D. 2018. High Gold Award
Performed by: Haley S. 2019. High Gold Award

WARM-UPS

(Walks on stage with a boombox)

Hello! My name is DJ Popeye and I have been hired to pump you up for your auditions here today! WOOOOOOOOOO! Who's excited?! I didn't hear you! Who's excited!?!?!? YEAH! Now, some of you might remember me from last year, or the year before that, or the year before that…or the…well, you get the idea. Like always, I have brought my trusty boombox which plays all the sickest beats for us to jelly jam and warm-up our instruments to. So, what do you say? Shall we get started?!

(BEAT)

WOOOOOOOO!!!

(Dramatically takes boombox, sets it down, presses play, gets into first position to dance. Nothing happens. Boombox doesn't start playing. Goes back to boombox, presses stop, presses play, gets back into his position. Nothing happens. They start to freak out on the boombox, they open the tape deck to find that the boombox has eaten the "sickest beats" cassette tape. They turn to audience and say…)

WOOOO!! Looks like my trusty boombox not only likes to play the "sickest beats" but it also likes to eat them. So, we'll have to change it up this year. I'll need your help to set up a beat. So, everyone, please, uhhh…slap your thighs like this. Then, clap your hands. Then, snap with your left hand and snap with your right. So it's…

(They show the motion. There should be four beats all together. Thighs, Clap, Snap, Snap. This sets up the beat for DJ Popeye to improv the following)

Okay, here we go, with the sickest beats known to mankind...

(To the tune of "Oops I Did It Again" by Britney Spears)

"Oops, she did it again. Not Britney Spears, because that's copyright infringement."

(BEAT)

WOOOOOO!!!!

Okay, well I think you guys are warmed up enough. Everyone break legs today. I'm going to go break my trusty boombox and start running music off of my phone. Until next time, DJ Popeye OUT!

Originally performed by: Noah D. 2020. High Gold Award
Best Actor Award

ABOUT THE AUTHOR

Gary Baker is an actor, writer, producer, and theatre instructor in North Florida. After years of writing original works for his students, he decided to share these works to help other students who might be having a hard time finding quality material for auditions or competitions.

RESOURCES

Awkward Break-In: https://youtu.be/hPCbHyLUdfc

Becky the Babysitter: https://youtu.be/ycAHiFTfHAE

Brother's Territory: https://youtu.be/yQeBRwE0sJM

Bunny Expectations: https://youtu.be/2J_liBA8Jac

Charm: https://youtu.be/OW35ZP7H1eA

Dislocated: https://youtu.be/qrU5Cx-HYRs

Double Dip: https://youtu.be/Onz4NwXgE9A

Emma: https://youtu.be/lZBKe0g7tos

Flirty: https://youtu.be/f0BsIEhpbT0

Fundraiser: https://youtu.be/5d1ob4t0PcA

History 101: https://youtu.be/gt4mGw6kCe0

Imaginary Friend Party: https://youtu.be/RLbIs39I5Vc

Investigator: https://youtu.be/d8t9JZIKKGQ
https://youtu.be/41VO12F5xCE

Loaf of Bread: https://youtu.be/Dj5jjFeKN04

Lola: https://youtu.be/PbirMIYIS3c

Play Practice: https://youtu.be/yg2SzQcE0GA

Slime: https://youtu.be/mOrgWk0ECss

Sports: https://youtu.be/fj6OG2zDoNc

Sprinkles: https://youtu.be/km7_Kdj4wzY

Sunshine Girl: https://youtu.be/DYk8597aioY

Theatre Etiquette: https://youtu.be/IsQTDhl8ZzA

The Funeral: https://youtu.be/EJlUGuloCEk

Tryouts: https://youtu.be/ZSsO6QYh2r4

Twins: https://youtu.be/bm_J86DMpsQ

Visiting Hours: https://youtu.be/bWWyq-6fHBw

Warm-ups: https://youtu.be/BQtzm-snrak

Made in the USA
Middletown, DE
27 June 2023